Project Cost Control
for Managers

Project Cost Control for Managers

Bill G. Tompkins
Doctor of Engineering
NRG Systems, Inc.

Gulf Publishing Company
Book Division
Houston, London, Paris, Tokyo

Acknowledgments

I affectionately acknowledge my wife, Robyn, for her patience and significant editorial and transcriptional assistance.

Additionally, I would like to acknowledge those managers and educators for whom I have worked and under whom I have studied for unselfishly contributing to my education and experience in order that I might understand and describe the concepts and relationships presented herein. The transfer of knowledge from one generation to the next is never painless.

Library of Congress Cataloging in Publication Data
Tompkins, Bill G.
  Project cost control for managers.
  Includes index.
  1. Cost control. 2. Industrial project management.
I. Title.
HD47.3.T66   1985   658.1'552   84-22443
ISBN 0-87201-684-6

Contents

Preface

The project cost control skills of management are usually acquired through experience, because educational institutions provide little academic coursework on the subject, and the success of a project cost control program depends primarily on the ability and experience of the top level of management. It is therefore necessary for executives, the general manager, and middle managers to understand the fundamentals of how project cost control relates to every department within a company. All too often management is under-involved in project cost control, thinking that such a program requires only rudimentary exercises for a cost engineer or scheduler. This results in historical data reporting rather than effective cost control. A project cost control program must have the participation of all levels of management, or it will not be successful.

This book addresses the most important role in project cost control—that of management. Up to now, managers had great difficulty in obtaining a clear, concise presentation of the fundamentals of project cost control aimed specifically at management. Therefore, this book presents this valuable information for use by management personnel, as well as those aspiring to attain management stature. The reader should have some background in project estimating, scheduling, accounting, and management to fully understand the concepts here. The book primarily addresses, through use of examples, project cost control as it relates to engineering and construction companies. However, the same fundamental concepts with slight modifications are applicable to operating and manufacturing companies. Such modifications have been suggested throughout the text. The information presented herein will not significantly change with time, thereby making the information excellent as a permanent reference document.

This book describes concepts and offers guidelines on their application. The reader is expected to apply these concepts to his or her specific situation. To accomplish this, the reader may need to adapt some of the concepts and forms presented and consult other publications referenced in the text.

The fundamentals of cost control are easy to understand; detailing of these fundamental concepts gives the appearance of complication. Considerable literature presenting a wealth of project schedule and cost control details is available to estimators, cost engineers, and schedulers who work with these details each day. Suggested references are listed in Chapter 6.

Bill G. Tompkins

Project Cost Control
for Managers

Chapter 1
"I Think We Have a
Cost Control Problem"

The content of this book will first be of interest, in many cases, when a manager experiences project budget overruns caused by a nonexistent or inadequate project cost control program. This is normal, because most inexperienced managers and employees tend to over-simplify the concepts of and need for cost management until they experience project cost overruns.

Usually, a company's top level of management first admits that the company has a cost control problem when consecutive projects consistently experience cost overruns. In most cases, the executive is still not sure a problem exists; therefore, the phrase, "I think we have a cost problem" is often used. Isolated cases of project overruns are usually justified in some manner and normally do not cause changes in whatever project cost control program that may exist. When consecutive project overruns first occur, a statistical connection between the overruns and type of project is explored, a possible explanation given, and again no procedural changes made. However, soon thereafter the situation deteriorates into an inability to adequately forecast gross profit and, eventually, net profit. This forecasting inability will quickly impact the accounting function, which, so it seems, is the final bastion with sufficient clout to initiate change. As the problem worsens, employees dealing with cost and schedule details have probably suggested numerous ways to improve the project cost control program but were unable to effect company change without management's backing. It is important to understand why this sequence of events typically occurs.

1

When a project begins, cost is the first concern, because the sales department or project estimator requires competitive costing and/or pricing in order to complete the sale or, in the case of an operating company, convince management to proceed. After the sale, cost immediately drops to a much lower position on the list of project priorities. Such priorities as schedule (getting the job done), safety, functional adequacy, operability, and maintainability become more important.

This situation is usually reinforced by the customer or user, since his cost concerns are now behind him. However, the cost considerations associated with project execution are yet to be experienced by management. How these cost challenges are handled will determine the profitability (e.g., corporate profit or return on investment) of each project.

The Profit Forecast Indicator

An inaccurate profit forecast ($> \pm 10\%$) is the first indicator of a problem and is usually what causes management to implement or change a project cost control program. Therefore, a brief discussion of the profit forecasting role in corporate decision making is necessary.

Profit forecasting begins with individual forecasting of actual project cost performance relative to the allotted project budget and ends with cumulative forecasts of corporate profit. These forecasts involve two project categories: projects in progress and potential projects. *This text addresses projects in progress only.* Based on the corporate profit forecasts, upper management plans financial distributions, such as stock dividends, bonuses, corporate participation in profit sharing and pension programs, capital expenditures for improvements or expansions; discharges loans; and performs other similar functions. The manner in which these financial distributions are handled will in turn affect corporate stock values and consequently investor attitudes. One of the most influential factors in investor attitudes is confidence in the company's management, which translates into investment security. Lack of investor confidence caused by inaccurate financial forecasting can easily cause stock prices to fall and possibly result in a change in upper management. Consequently, if management has not had the courage or initiative to implement or change a project cost control program, significant inaccuracy in corporate financial forecasting will provide that initiative.

Profit forecasting begins at the project level. The project manager with the assistance of the project cost engineer and scheduler predict (or forecast) future project expenditures. A technique for determining and recording such forecasts is covered in Chapters 4, 6, and 7. The historical project expenditures and predicted expenditures are compared to the project budget resulting in a predicted project cost over- or underrun. These predictions for each project are accumulated resulting in a predicted (or forecast) corporate project cost over- or underrun. These project forecast values distributed over a preset time period become influential values in the corporate financial forecast. Exactly how the project forecast values are involved in the corporate forecast is determined by the accounting technique used. Consequently, the project forecast at the lowest level becomes the first building block in the corporate financial forecast pyramid.

Perhaps a reader's first response to this building block concept may be somewhat analogous to that of voting (i.e., "I determine only one forecast value, therefore it won't make much difference.") Another ill-conceived approach is that of extremely conservative project forecasting (i.e., "If I forecast conservatively the worst that can happen is that the project underruns, which is good news to everyone.") Adoption of either of these two attitudes at any corporate level where predictions are developed will significantly contribute to inaccuracy of financial forecasts. Any error in the lowest level predicted values (i.e., first pyramid building block) is compounded when values are summed as the corporate forecast is developed. There is room for argument that these errors may be offsetting rather than compounding. This is even a worse situation because now the percent error in the final values cannot be estimated with any accuracy. Consequently, it is extremely important that the lowest-level predicted values (usually determined or approved by each project manager) be as accurate as possible. A reasonable expectation is $\pm$ 10%. Intentional or known errors in excess of this range easily lead to loss of confidence in the project cost control program.

A more detailed discussion of financial forecasting, which includes profit forecasting and the impact of accuracy, is included in many books covering management and/or accounting.

How to Regain Control of Project Costs

If company forecasts indicate a cost control problem, how can management regain control? This book describes one successful management technique used in controlling project costs. However, to fully understand and accurately use the technique, the reader should first read the book in its entirety and then return to those areas of most interest.

To ensure that project costs are important employee concerns, management should first initiate a company project cost control program. This program must include the required contribution of each department or project function. Rudiments of internal procedures may need to be reviewed to assure compliance with the program; however, the program should not dictate how each department or project functional area performs its work. The task of initiating and enforcing a project cost control program must not be handed down to line employees. For proper emphasis, these functions must be handled by management.

A project cost control program is manifested in a work flow procedure, not in a list of historical budget and cost data compiled manually or with the use of a computer program (a common misconception). The effective program provides a balance between two extremes: the oversimplified and the over-controlled approaches. The over-simplified approach to project cost control (analogous to balancing the family checkbook) is viewed as a spare time accounting activity involving simple addition and subtraction. The over-controlled approach is exemplified by a cumbersome procedure that costs more than any possible savings such a program could provide. The optimum balance between these two approaches is different for each company, and must be determined by management. Chapter 2 describes a program (using the "RIICH Technique") that exhibits this optimum balance.

One important obstacle to the success of any project cost control program is the existence of language barriers. All employees assume they speak the same language. Eventually, they learn that each discipline has its own terminology. Each employee endeavors to define the company's main business interests in terms of his discipline, thereby providing rationale as to why his terminology should be exclusively adopted internally. Many times precedence is relied on to establish terminology definitions. An effective approach to this dilemma is discussed in Chapter 3.

Chapter 4, Work Flow Path Fundamentals, discusses the procedural philosophy of work flow, and presents concepts upon which a successful project cost control program properly functions. When the fundamentals presented in this chapter are followed, the program will automatically converge presale project estimates with after-completion project costs. This maximizes profit through protection of planned margins and the existence of budget underruns. Also, historical project data become credible and valuable.

A subtle but formidable obstruction in the path of program success is the entrenched numbering system. As the company grows, departmental numbering systems are established. These systems are usually arbitrary relative to any overall company numbering system requirements. Because successful project cost control requires the efficient exchange of information from one department to another, some compatibility between numbering systems (related to interdepartmental work flow) will eventually be required. This awesome task is discussed in Chapter 5.

Project schedule/estimate considerations, as they relate to project cost control, are discussed in Chapter 6. The hidden cost of schedule slippage is a menace associated with every project. Schedule slippage directly results in extra project cost. This cost overrun is difficult to detect as it occurs, and is usually ignored, justified with the "makeup syndrome." There are methods for avoiding these overruns. Since all projects begin with a project estimate and are carried out within the framework of this estimate, several estimating considerations are important to overall project cost control. The makeup syndrome associated with expenditure justification can be as devastating to control budgets as the hidden cost of schedule slippage. Again, there are methods for avoiding these overruns.

Last and very important to project cost control, is data handling, reporting, and use, as discussed in Chapter 7. This final program phase provides management with sufficient information to close the "control feedback loop." The makeup syndrome, as it applies to costs, may also be experienced in this phase.

This book sequentially discusses in detail the company interrelationship fundamentals required to develop and implement a successful project cost control program. A manager, due to time and priority constraints, does not typically become involved in the detailed execution (e.g., schedule details) of program documents. Therefore, the text does not attempt to establish detail procedures for any one project functional area or department. However, an example chart of accounts and example project cost control forms are offered in Appendices A and B, respectively.

Chapter 2
Cost Control—Who Needs It?

The most important aspect in determining who needs a project cost control program is understanding the definition of cost control. A popular misconception within industry is that use of a computer program for cost reporting is synonymous with cost control. While a cost control program may require a computer for data manipulation and handling, an effective program consists of an integrated system of work flow and paperwork paths that direct daily design and construction project efforts. These paths incorporate the efforts of all project functions, thereby providing the following cost control features:

☐ A system of checks and balances, automatically requiring that the finished product has the same characteristics as that which was sold or initiated.
☐ Easy access to current project data in order to assess the project status at any time.
☐ Easy comparison of project progress with current expenditures.
☐ Minimization of cost overruns through early detection and project redirection.

The integrated work flow and paperwork paths are usually described in a set of company procedures. Due to its importance, project cost control should itself be one of those procedures. Consequently, a project cost control program is, in actuality, a work flow procedure.

To provide the previously listed cost control features, a project cost control program must involve every corporate employee in some manner. Consequently, project communication is very important; however, there is one critical communication link (i.e., between sales and project management), as depicted in Figure 2-1. Due to the basic structure of most companies, there tends to be a natural physical and functional separation between those personnel who conceptualize and initiate a project (i.e., sales) and those who implement and complete the job (i.e., project management). As illustrated, the communication link between sales and project management is the most important for the financial success of any project. Each of these two project functions must accurately communicate either planned profit margins or project cost under-

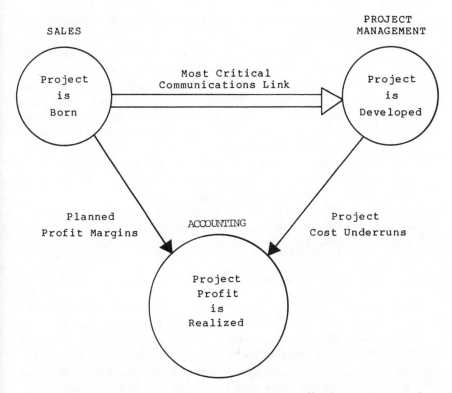

Figure 2-1. Basic corporate communications affecting cost control.

runs to the corporate accounting function. However, communication of what was planned during sale of the project (e.g., project estimate) and the constant, daily comparison of what was planned to activities in progress (e.g., expenditures for design, procurement, fabrication, and/ or construction) are very important to project financial success.

As briefly discussed in Chapter 1, there are two extreme approaches to a project cost control program: the over-simplified and the over-controlled. The over-simplified approach consists of charging the corporate accounting function with periodic reporting of project budgets less current expenditures or cost commitments. This approach can only provide historical data with no opportunity for cost control. The over-controlled approach relies on a complicated project cost control program that costs more to implement and use than the program can possibly save. This type of program typically consists of time and expense reporting in excess of that reasonably possible by employees (e.g., less than one hour increments and costs less than those percentages discussed later). Excessive employee time reporting may also include detailed explanation of each hour spent on a project (e.g., piping design by individual pipe run). The optimum balance between these two extremes is different for each company. Therefore, the project cost control program for each company must be custom designed. Figure 2–2, discussed in greater detail later, provides a guideline for avoiding the over-simplified approach to project cost control. The "1% Rule" provides a guideline for avoiding the over-controlled approach. This rule states that an item or task cost amounting to less than 1% of its primary account (see Appendix A— General Chart of Accounts) should be controlled as a sub-group, whose value is greater than 1% of its primary account, rather than individually. The cost to control project expenditures less than 1% will be greater than any potential savings. An example general chart of accounts exhibiting three account levels is discussed in Chapter 3.

To provide the optimum project cost control program for each specific application, management typically asks two questions: "Do we need it?" and "How should the program be developed?"

Do We Need It?

When starting a company, the new manager's time is primarily consumed by sales activities. However, as this early phase passes, he finds that he has to participate in completing the work sold, since the ability to continuously support employees on a long-term basis is still in doubt. During this time, projects seem somehow to be miraculously completed on time and under budget. Consequently, the attitude develops: "An expensive cost control program . . . who needs it?"

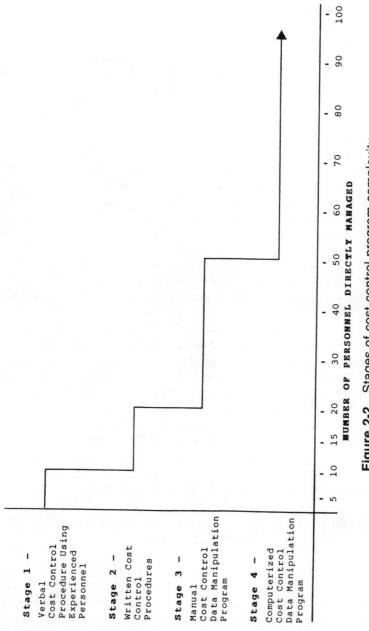

Figure 2-2. Stages of cost control program complexity.

As the company grows, the managers begin to assume more administrative roles with less involvement in other areas, and cost overruns begin. Consequently, the feeling becomes: "A cost control program . . . are we among those who need it?" This situation typically evolves because the initial personnel are highly motivated and highly experienced in project design and construction. Therefore, cost control is inherent in their daily activities. However, each of these initial employees probably learned the fundamentals of cost control through previous association with another company's cost control program. With company growth, new employees are normally not as motivated or experienced. Consequently, cost overruns result.

There is no indicator that dictates when a project cost control program should be implemented in order to avoid these initial cost overruns. Certainly, once cost overruns are experienced, it becomes obvious to management that some measure of control is needed. The relationship between the number of employees directly managed and the need for and complexity of a cost control program, as depicted in Figure 2-2, is the most accurate barometer. Other variables, such as sales revenue, sales/cost ratio, and manpower/material ratio, may impact the decision to implement a project cost control program. However, their combined influence is less significant than the number of employees directly managed.

There is some justification to stressing that a construction effort involves control of material costs, whereas a design effort involves control of only manpower costs. However, this material involvement requires more employees, therefore the need for a cost control program is still primarily influenced by the number of personnel directly managed, which includes direct employees, contract personnel, etc. who receive direct daily instruction from management. Personnel employed by a subcontractor should not be included. Figure 2-2 is a guideline showing when each of the four stages of a cost control program are typically needed. Cost tradeoff of manual data manipulation versus computer data manipulation is reflected in Stage 4 of Figure 2-2.

Developing Your Project Cost Control Program Using The "RIICH" Technique

There are several project cost control procedures marketed; however, no one procedure will totally satisfy a company's needs. It is highly probable that a commercially available program that is totally adopted will provide only historical data involving after-the-fact information, with no opportunity for cost control, or an "over-kill" whereby the program itself costs more than it could possibly save. Consequently, to be successful, management must develop a cost control program customized to the peculiarities of the company. A five-step technique used for developing this customized project cost control program is the Review, Integrate, Implement, Computerize, and Habit (i.e., RIICH) technique. This technique uses those portions of existing company procedures that are acceptable to develop the project cost control program. This limits the number of necessary procedural changes. Therefore, the program will be more easily and quickly adopted by employees because it is something they want to do, rather than something they have to do. Employee acceptance is a big factor in making the program work.

Step 1—Review

The company's existing cost and schedule control procedure is thoroughly reviewed. Although these procedures are not always in written form, they do exist as a daily work flow pattern. This daily work flow pattern should be flow charted (see the suggested project cost control program work flow discussed in Chapter 4). Care should be taken to depict the actual work flow path and not what employees feel the path should be. Also, it should be remembered that a work flow path described in an existing written procedure may not be presently in use. In essence, the work flow path that is in use should be flow charted. Since this step is carried out primarily through employee interviews, it may be difficult but not impossible to chart this actual work flow path. It is important to include all check and balance loops, decision points, and approval stages (as they presently exist) in the paths charted. The work flow charts should be categorized in the two areas of project responsibility (e.g., sales and project management) and formally distributed to upper management for discussion. This will provide the baseline on which necessary procedural changes will be made.

Step 2—Integration

The company's cost control procedure presently in use is now integrated with the cost control fundamentals presented in Chapter 4. The work flow charts developed in Step 1 are modified to reflect those cost control fundamentals not included. Typically, necessary modifications will constitute a 20 to 30% change in the work flow paths; however, this will be a function of the experience of the company's personnel. The proposed work flow path modifications should be clearly indicated on the charts developed in Step 1 and again formally distributed to upper management for discussion. At this time, preparation of a written cost control procedure begins. Once the work flow paths are agreed to by management, the cost control procedure can be finalized. This procedure must include the project cost control requirements for every department (or project function) in the company, since each department will have some cost control responsibility. Effective procedures include the basic check and balance loop, decision point, and approval stage fundamentals for project cost control. Otherwise, a historical cost data reporting system may be the only product of this exercise.

Step 3—Implementation

The project cost control procedure created in Step 2 is then implemented, which includes distributing the formal project cost control procedure, orienting and training personnel, and assisting all employees in applying the procedure to the first project. Reconciling the cost data reporting technique with the present accounting general ledger system, if not completed in Step 2, must be finalized at this time. Once the program is implemented, the work flow paths will begin to automatically adjust the final product characteristics to that which was sold. Additionally, the program allows for project-in-progress cost adjustments, increased emphasis on budget underruns, and credible historical data for estimating future projects. At this point, all project cost control data are manipulated manually to produce the required reports.

Step 4—Computerization (as needed)

With company growth comes project cost control data handling problems. Management should not immediately assume that a computer program is necessary. For small groups of personnel, data manipulation can be more economically handled manually. Once the decision to computerize is made, however, the possibility of developing a customized computer program for the cost control procedure should be investigated and compared with the cost and benefits of using available "canned" programs. Typically, "canned" computer programs provide a total capability. However, many of the benefits of this total capability are never used, but are part of the program use costs. Whereas, the cost of developing a customized computer program may be very economical.

Step 5—Habit

Once the project cost control program (consisting of the project cost control procedure and data handling technique) is implemented, cost control, ideally, will become an unconscious habit. Personnel will follow established work flow routines in accordance with the program. Since the program causes the automatic daily comparison of sales and project management information, thereby refining the product produced, the program results in a convergence of project cost and budget as shown in Figure 2-3. As illustrated, when a project begins, project cost forecasts (i.e., predictions) are somewhat greater than the budgeted values primarily due to the involvement of a new group of personnel. As the project progresses and this daily comparison is made, project cost forecasts converge with the project budget and actual costs. Depending on the accuracy of the estimate, upon which the project budget is based, this convergence may occur above or below the actual project budget. Addi-

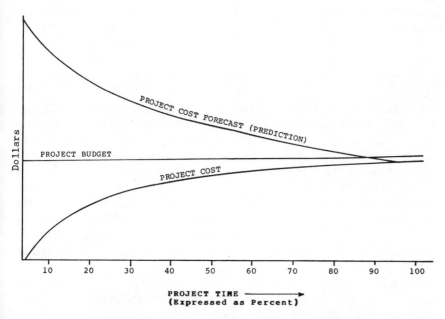

Figure 2-3. Project cost/budget convergence.

tionally, the historical data collected from use of the program will continually converge toward the actual required costs to produce a given product. This is the desired long-term result of such a program.

Summary

Using the five-step RIICH technique, an effective project cost control program can be developed and implemented. And, most importantly, it can be widely accepted by employees who, in turn, will guarantee its success. An example of an application of the RIICH technique in conjunction with material from Chapter 4 is presented in Appendix C.

The Cost Control Group

Once the need for a project cost control program has been accepted and the optimum program developed using the RIICH technique, the next question management must answer is, "Who should perform those tasks associated with administration of the project cost control program?" These tasks will involve data collection, review, manipulation, reporting, and management consultation. Should these activities be absorbed by the existing accounting function, or should a special group dedicated to this effort be established? This question must be answered by examining the potential savings that may result from the cost control program.

For initial projects using the program, it is possible to save 10 to 20% of the project budget if the program is properly administered. Through application on subsequent projects, the potential savings is less, since the program automatically causes the convergence of project estimates and control budgets. However, a minimum of 5% savings is possible on any project. These potential savings must be compared to manpower costs in order to determine if a dedicated cost control group is economically justified. However, it is important to remember that without the use of a project cost control program, cost overruns on a runaway project may reach 200 to 300% of the project budget before control can be established.

The accounting function may perform the project cost control program administrative duties, since they are more attuned to financial reporting and associated deadlines. However, accounting personnel typically do not have the background required to verify the accuracy of a line item description. Consequently, this may lead to inaccuracies in the cost control program reports. On the other hand, a cost control group (or department) typically consists of cost engineers who are trained in correctly identifying project items and tasks. However, this approach is more costly and tends to be used only for larger projects or groups of projects that provide sufficient savings potential to cover these costs. The size of any cost control group should be in direct relationship with project potential savings.

One approach used quite frequently is to assign the administrative duties of the program to the accounting function until sufficient project savings are possible to support a cost control group. Obviously, adding accounting personnel to perform the new administrative duties is the same as adding personnel to establish a cost control group and must be viewed in that manner. When addition of personnel is necessary, these new employees should be cost engineers administratively reporting to a technical department manager. A second important feature of using this approach is that the project cost control program details must be developed by management in coordination with departmental functions, but not by any one department.

Chapter 3
Bridging the Language Barrier

One of the singularly most important problems confronting any company is communication, its frequency, accuracy, and interpretation. To accomplish effective communication, all parties must have a similar understanding of the definition of key words and phrases. Each discipline involved in a project (e.g., sales, engineering, accounting, purchasing, etc.) has developed, through different educational and experiential exposure, a separate definition of some cost control terms. The most common occurrence of this communication breakdown is when an accountant participates in a project design meeting, or an engineer participates in a financial meeting. After each of these meetings, it is normal to hear of either employee's lack of understanding (or interest) of what was discussed. Another example is the continuing struggle of any one corporate department to require that all other departments in the company adopt their terminology. Rationale offered includes statements such as:

"All that matters is the bottom line (i.e., profit); therefore, all employees should learn accounting terminology."

"This is an engineering/construction company, not an accounting company; therefore, all employees should learn engineering terminology."

"Nothing happens until we make a sale; therefore, all employees should learn the sales terminology."

Consequently, the race is on by each department to set terminology precedence. This type of competitive activity between disciplines is counter productive to the company business goals.

In verbal and nonverbal communication, the language dictionary plays a major role by providing definitions of terms. Therefore, it is necessary to provide a "dictionary," (i.e., glossary of terms) that defines and clarifies cost control terms. A second communication aid, the general chart of accounts, is also developed to assign a numerical identifier to specific cost items or tasks. This identifier provides an easy line item reference. The intent of these two documents is to bridge the language barrier between disciplines and/or corporate departments.

Glossary of Cost Control Terms

Many cost control terms may presently be listed in a language dictionary. However, a dictionary presents all of the various word definitions as they relate to the different applications. For a specific application (i.e., project cost control) reference to a language dictionary is confusing and non-conclusive. Therefore, a list of project cost control terms with associated definitions is offered to provide definitions for the majority of terms used when carrying out a typical project cost control program. As the reader uses the RIICH technique described in Chapter 2 to develop and implement the optimum program for his company, the glossary of terms should be expanded to include any terms peculiar to that application. The intent of the glossary is to provide a clear definition for terms frequently used by all disciplines involved in a project cost control program in a manner that requires no previous training.

The user may directly adopt the glossary presented herein or make modifications or additions as he feels necessary to more accurately reflect the details of his company's operations. In either case the glossary must be continually expanded and refined as a company grows in order to accurately reflect the current intended use of the project cost control program.

Account Code—The numerical identifier established for a project item or task using the general chart of accounts as a guide.

Actual Completion—The percent (%) completed of a task at a given time during project execution.

Actual Cost—The total of all project expenditures committed or paid including labor, materials, transporation, etc. that are directly resulting from project effort.

Applied Costs—Sometimes called *Direct Costs*. All expenditures (including manpower costs) directly chargeable to projects.

Approved Change Order—A customer change order that has been completed, submitted to the customer, and approved by the customer.

Authorization for Expenditure (AFE)—Information presented on the appropriate form to management for approval justifying an expenditure.

Bid Package—See *Request for Quotation.*

Bid Tab—A tabulation of competitive quotation salient points arranged to permit comparative analysis for compliance with specifications and lowest price. This activity leads to the selection of the successful bidder.

Budget Portion—The summed value of those current control budget items or tasks that have been committed. This value provides management with a value to compare with committed amount to determine current overrun/underrun status.

Capital Expenditure—An operating cost for acquiring property or equipment that is not directly chargeable to a project.

Committed Capital—Project expenditures for which written purchase orders or contracts have been issued.

Committed Freight—The freight expenditure (i.e., compensation paid for transportation) for the committed capital (as applicable).

Committed Quantity—The item quantity reflected in the committed capital. This value should be in the same units of measure as the initial control quantity.

Contingency—That funding included in the project estimate to cover costs which may be encountered during project execution and are difficult to identify while preparing the project estimate.

Control Budget—A project financial breakdown developed from the project estimate, used as the basis for control of project spending.

Cost Center—A company subdivision (e.g., division or department) established for the purpose of cost allocation and accumulation against which financial performance is evaluated.

Cost Forecast—The predicted total cost of an item or project usually developed by the project manager with assistance from the project cost control engineer.

Current Control Budget—The current project budget including all customer change orders presently approved (in writing).

Customer Change Orders—Changes to the project that have been described on the appropriate form and submitted to the customer for approval.

Delivery Date—The date the purchased item is scheduled for delivery. The promised delivery date is the date the vendor promised the item would be received by the purchaser. The predicted delivery date is the date the project manager anticipates receipt of the item.

Direct Cost—Costs that are directly chargeable to a project such as labor and materials.

Escalation—Historical or projected cost increases over a specific period of time, usually expressed as rate of change.

Exception Reporting—Reporting of only those line items of a project that are forecast to overrun the budgeted cost.

Estimate—See *Project Estimate.*

Extra Work Order (EWO)—An item of work outside and independent of the original contract, and not required to fulfill the terms of the contract.

General Chart of Accounts—A listing of items or tasks involved in a project by categories, thereby providing a standardized listing to be used for cost control. The general chart of accounts consists of the primary, secondary, and tertiary accounts.

Gross Margin—The project sales price minus the applied or direct costs.

Historical Cost Report—The final project cost report after project completion. Detailed in accordance with the general chart of accounts.

Indirect Costs—See *Overhead Costs.*

Initial Control Budget—Sometimes called the *Definitive Project Estimate.* The current estimated costs of a project immediately after the sale. This value is closely related to the initial control quantity.

Initial Control Quantity—The item quantity reflected in the Initial Control Budget.

Labor Burden Costs—Unapplied (indirect) costs associated with payroll (e.g., vacation pay, employee benefits, FICA tax, etc.).

Line Item—A discrete item for purchase or project task to occur on a specific project. Line items for each project are detailed in accordance with the general chart of accounts.

Material Requisition (MR)—A request on the appropriate form to obtain vendor's or subcontractors's quotations and/or to issue purchase orders or subcontracts for same.

Material Take-Off (MTO)—A detailed listing of materials compiled from drawings or other design documentation.

Monthly Cost and Progress Report—A series of project reports for the comparison of cost and progress data. Issued at various summary levels in accordance with the intended reader.

Net Income—The portion of the revenue remaining after deducting all applied and unapplied costs and taxes.

Net Margin—The gross margin minus the unapplied costs.

Overhead Costs—Sometimes called *Indirect Costs.* Expenditures, other than applied or direct, that are basic to doing business (e.g., office rental, utilities, supplies, administrative, and sales).

Overrun/Underrun—The amount that is greater/less than the project control budget for the project task or item.

Planned Completion—The percent (%) of a task, at a given time during project execution, that was to be completed in accordance with the initial project schedule.

Postmortem—A complete project financial analysis from time of inception to completion once a project is complete (i.e., after all project costs have been incurred).

Project Cost Forecast—The total predicted project item or task cost at any given time during the execution of a project.

Project Estimate—An estimate of project costs based on historical data, accumulated for tendering a proposal. There are two types:

☐ *Order of Magnitude*—Project estimate based on a conceptual definition of project design and scope of work.

☐ *Preliminary Project Estimate*—Based on definite design specifications and scope of work.

Project Schedule—The schedule developed within the framework of the proposal schedule for continuously monitoring project progress.

Proposal Schedule—The preliminary project schedule defining major milestones, developed for tendering a proposal.

Purchase Order—An authorization to a vendor to furnish and deliver specific materials or equipment and a commitment to pay the specified amount.

Request for Quotation (RFQ)—An invitation to submit a quotation for furnishing services, material, or equipment. Also referred to as *Request for Proposal (RFP)*, *Tender Request*, *Request for Tenders*, or *Bid Package*.

Revenue—Any income from a source outside the company.

Scope of Work—A description of services, material, and equipment to be provided by the company. This description may contain design details, capacities, etc.

Subcontract—An agreement between one party to a prime contract and a third party for some specified portion of work and a commitment to pay the specified amount.

Subcontractor—A provider of services for such tasks as design and construction operating under a contract arrangement.

Supplier—See *Vendor*.

Task—A defined activity of work to be accomplished on a project.

Trending—A project cost and schedule control technique used continuously through all stages of a project to illustrate deviations from the control budget or project schedule. Reporting of trends (or deviations) offers management the opportunity to make project decisions in advance of commitments.

Unapplied Costs—Sometimes called *Indirect Costs*. All expenditures (including manpower costs) not directly chargeable to projects. These costs include overhead and labor burden.

Vendor—A product supplier or fabricator operating under a purchase order arrangement; sometimes called *Supplier.*

Voucher—An accounting form to which bills and receipts are attached showing the authorization for the payment, the specifics for settlement, and other details. The voucher may also be used to correct an entry to the general ledger.

Work Code—A set of numbers (codes) assigned to work functions to identify the type of manpower to be used or spent on a project. Work codes are used in scheduling and time reporting activities.

General Chart of Accounts

This document is necessary to provide a numerical identifier to project cost control program item or task costs in order to enhance project team intercommunication. The general chart of accounts provides a guideline for assigning these identifiers. If the item description is confusing or vague to the user, the item can be referred to by its numerical identifier. An example general chart of accounts is presented in Appendix A. This example uses a three-level approach to providing project cost summaries: primary, secondary, and tertiary account codes. Project detail is entered at the tertiary level and summarized to the secondary and primary levels for management review. The general chart of accounts in Appendix A has been structured specifically so that project events (i.e., tasks), which are represented by line items in the control budget, occur in the same sequence as their line item identifiers represent. This principle is mostly applicable to the primary account codes. For example, as indicated by the sequence of numbers 1 through 7 (Appendix A), project management (1) begins first, followed immediately by engineering and design (2). Next, purchasing of equipment and material (3) follows. The shop fabrication and assembly (4) activity is next followed by inspection and testing (5), and packaging/crating, loading and transportation (6). The final project event is field construction (7). This sequence is representative of most projects. However, the reader may wish to make modifications to this task sequence to assure that his sequential tasks are numbered in an ascending manner. This relationship between the task numbering and event occurrence becomes more important as the project progresses. The task numbers provide a subtle reference for all employees to the present status of project progress. This indicator cannot be directly quantified but is another use of easily available techniques to provide a project with a logical, uniform method for handling information and check and balance on progress and cost status.

The general chart of accounts is a guideline for developing the project estimate (as discussed in Chapter 6) during the sales phase of a project. Prior to the design phase of a project, the general chart of accounts is used as a guideline to expand the project estimate into the initial control budget. During the remainder of a project, the general chart of accounts provides the guideline for maintaining the current control budget. Once a project cost item or task is initially assigned a general chart of accounts numerical identifier, the item or task identifier and initial budget value is never changed throughout the project.

Additionally, the general chart of accounts provides commonality between projects, thereby allowing for historical cost comparisons. Comparisons can also be made between historical project cost data and current project estimates for future projects with confidence that there were no omissions.

The general chart of accounts is not intended to be a cookbook procedure for project cost control. Instead, it is a categorical guideline for identifying individual project items or tasks. This approach improves the value of historical data and standardizes identification of project elements. If a secondary or tertiary level category or item description does not exist in the example general chart of accounts, it should be added as necessary to conform to the needs of the application. However, the primary account codes should never be altered, because this account code level provides an industry-wide standard of comparison against which project estimate accuracy may be evaluated.

Accurate project historical data not only show project financial performance, but also provide data for future project estimates. Using the project cost summary form shown in Appendix B, the project estimate (Column #1) is initially approved for project sale. The project actual cost (Column #2) remains blank until the project is completed. At that time, Column #1 is updated to include all project change orders, and Column #2, project cost, is also completed thereby providing a historical comparison of budgeted and committed costs. These data are extremely important in preparing project estimates for future proposals. More important than historical budget/committed comparison data is the percentage data entered to the right (in each column) of the cost data. After completion of several projects using this approach, the percent represented by the cost of each primary account will begin to form a pattern. Management's knowledge of these historical percentages will assist in judging the accuracy of new project estimates. However, the percentages should not be used in reverse in order to estimate a project. A rigorous cost buildup (i.e., project estimate) procedure should always be used for initial project estimates.

Chapter 4
Work Flow Path Fundamentals

During the initial growth period of a new company, management primarily depends on the experience of the few key employees to control project costs. Management gradually realizes, with the first occurrence of project cost overruns, that the percentage of experienced, cost-conscious employees decreases with company growth. Therefore, management initiates a project cost control program, or adopts the program used by the parent company. Subsequently, the program never seems to adequately fulfill the corporate needs, and may gradually evolve into a cumbersome system that costs more to maintain than it can possibly save. This usually results from a lack of experience within the initial personnel in the techniques of cost control.

To ensure that the first project cost control program developed fulfills the company's needs, management should follow the guidelines offered in this chapter, which establish the minimum requirements for controlling project costs. The "fundamental concepts" presented are intentionally general in certain areas, allowing management some latitude to deal with special circumstances, which occur on every project. A rigid cookbook procedure for project cost control is not practical. This chapter is intended as a guideline to assure that project costs are under control without hampering creative design work.

The first phase of every project is the sales effort. This effort may consist of selling a proposed project to another company or, in the case of an operating company, selling the idea to management. Once a project is sold, completion of the remaining effort (i.e., engineering, purchasing, construction) should coincide closely with what was intended during the sale phase, unless changes are clearly documented. Therefore, the communication link between the sales effort and project management is the most critical one affecting cost control for the duration of the project. The efficiency of this communication link can potentially generate project profit/savings through budget underruns in excess of the planned profit margin. This goal is the first priority of every project manager. However, it must be noted that field rework caused by the purchase of poor quality services or materials can easily absorb earlier budget underruns. Consequently, the trade-off between budget savings and a quality product involves experienced judgment by the project manager.

Efficient communication between sales and project management requires that specific work flow paths plus effective checks and balances be established through project cost control procedures. The flow charts presented in this chapter are intended as an overview of these work flow paths, thereby providing an understandable, "at-a-glance" reference. The reader may easily determine work flow requirements by referring to the appropriate flow chart. The current position on the work flow path may then be determined for any given effort. Tasks remaining to complete the effort are then easily identified.

A typical engineering and construction company organizational chart establishing function or departmental titles is presented in Figure 4-1. Figures 4-2 and 4-3 diagramatically depict sales work flow paths. Figures 4-4 through 4-6 depict project management work flow paths.

The following two sections offer detailed discussion of sales and project management functions, respectively. Example project cost control forms referenced in this and other chapters are presented in Appendix B.

Sales Function

Using a typical engineering and construction company as an example, the sales function usually reports directly to the general manager. Therefore, the sales manager and manager of proposals are ultimately responsible for the sales effort, including project cost control requirements. The project development effort for this function is subdivided into two phases—the proposal phase and the after-sale phase. Work flow paths for these two phases of the sales function are shown in Figures 4-2 and 4-3. In essence, the project cost control responsibility associated with the sales function begins with development of the project estimate, which evolves into the initial control budget, shown in Figure 4-7. Once project management accepts responsibility for the project, the sales function assists project management by verifying the budget value

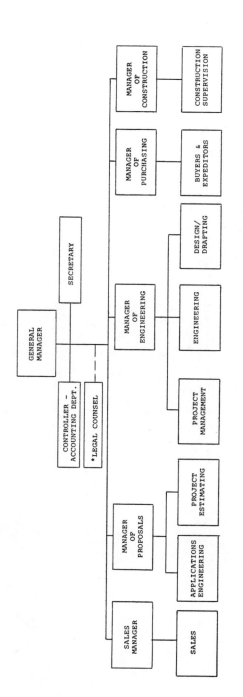

Figure 4-1. Typical organizational chart.

* Not permanent staff

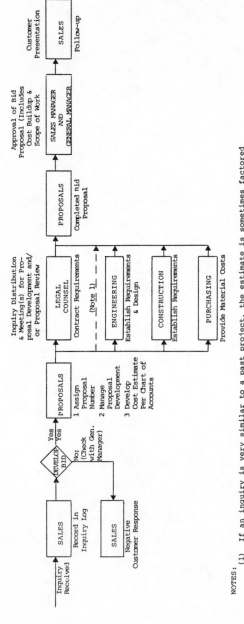

Figure 4-2. Sales work flow path—Proposal phase.

NOTES: (1)   If an inquiry is very similar to a past project, the estimate is sometimes factored from previous historical project cost data and the proposal developed without the assistance of other departments.

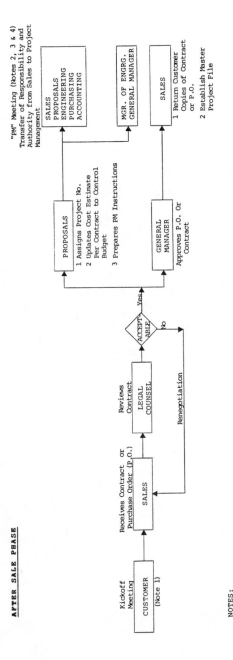

AFTER SALE PHASE

Kickoff Meeting

CUSTOMER (Note 1)

Receives Contract or Purchase Order (P.O.)

SALES

Reviews Contract

LEGAL COUNSEL

Renegotiation

ACCEPTABLE — Yes / No

PROPOSALS

1 Assigns Project No.
2 Updates Cost Estimate Per Contract to Control Budget
3 Prepares PM Instructions

GENERAL MANAGER

Approves P.O. Or Contract

"PM" Meeting (Notes 2, 3 & 4)
Transfer of Responsibility and Authority from Sales to Project Management

SALES
PROPOSALS
ENGINEERING
PURCHASING
ACCOUNTING

MGR. OF ENGRG.
GENERAL MANAGER

SALES

1 Return Customer Copies of Contract or P.O.

2 Establish Master Project File

Figure 4-3. Sales work flow path—After sale phase.

NOTES:

(1) Does not occur for each project.

(2) Project Management (PM) Instructions includes a written Transmittal, Control Budget, Proposal, Contract or P.O. and Customer Specifications, as a minimum. Upon acceptance (within two weeks) of the PM Instructions by the Manager of Engineering, the PM Instructions Transmittal is signed and returned to Sales.

(3) This may not be a formal meeting; all material may be handed directly to the Manager of Engineering.

(4) A copy of the PM Instructions is retained by Proposals in order to provide a budget check, per Figure 3-5.

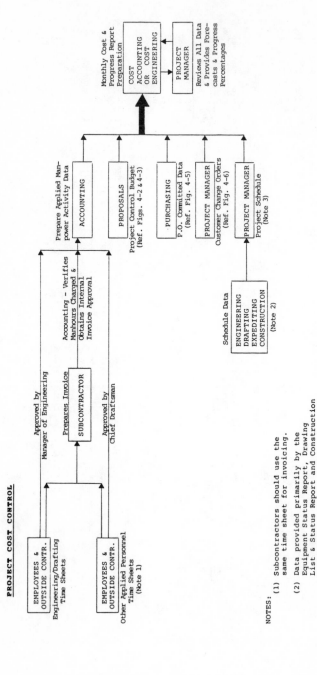

Figure 4-4. Project management work flow path—Project cost control.

PROJECT COST CONTROL

NOTES: (1) Subcontractors should use the same time sheet for invoicing.

(2) Data provided primarily by the Equipment Status Report, Drawing List & Status Report and Construction Reports.

(3) Project Manager may use a simple bar chart or one of the computer CPM techniques.

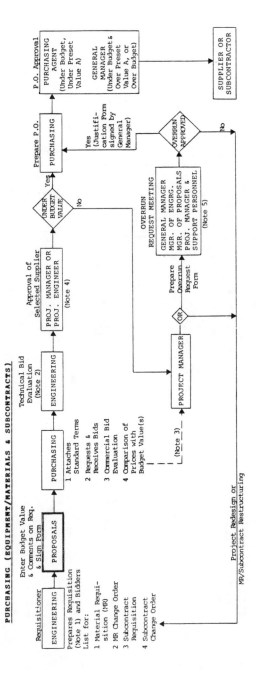

Figure 4-5. Project management work flow path—Purchasing (equipment/materials and subcontracts).

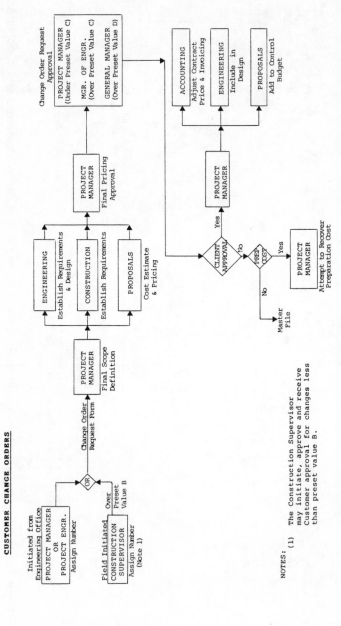

Figure 4-6. Project management work flow path—customer change orders.

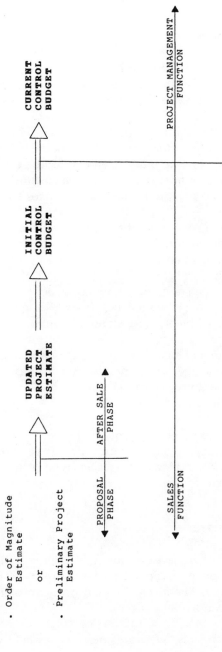

Figure 4-7. Control budget evolution.

of project items or tasks as project management requests expenditure authorization for each. *This assistance is a critical link in project success.*

Proposal Phase

This phase of project development (Figure 4-2) covers the time between the receipt of the customer inquiry and final sale. The following sequence of events describes the work flow paths:

☐ The customer inquiry is received by the sales department and placed in the sales log. A management decision is made regarding whether to tender a proposal. If management decides not to tender a proposal, the sales department responds to the customer accordingly. If a proposal is to be prepared, the inquiry passes to the proposals department.

☐ The proposals department assigns a proposal number, manages proposal development, and develops a project estimate in accordance with the general chart of accounts. The proposal may be developed totally from historical project data, or with the assistance of other departments, such as engineering, construction, and purchasing. However, legal counsel should be involved in every proposal to assure compliance with corporate standard contract terms. The project estimate may take one of two forms: order of magnitude or preliminary project estimate, as defined in the glossary in Chapter 3.

☐ The sales manager and general manager must approve the proposal document and project estimate before the completed proposal is presented to the customer.

The project cost summary and the three project detail estimate forms (Forms B-1 through B-4 in Appendix B) may be used to prepare the Project Estimate. An explanation of each type of form entry is presented with each form.

After-Sale Phase

This phase of project development (Figure 4-3) covers the time between sale of the project and transfer of project responsibility from sales to project management. The following sequence of events describes the after-sale phase work flow paths:

☐ For some projects, a "kickoff meeting" is held with the customer to assure that project management is fully aware of the customer's requirements. The signed contract may be received during this meeting. In some cases, the company may start work on the project based on a letter of intent.

□ Once the contract is received by the sales department, it is passed to legal counsel for review. If the contract terms are not acceptable, the contract should be returned to the sales department for renegotiation. If the contract terms are acceptable, two parallel activities occur.

□ The general manager reviews and approves the contract as the first parallel effort. The appropriate contract copies are returned to the customer by the sales department. Additionally, the sales department establishes the project master file. All project data, paperwork, etc. resulting from the project is routed to and retained in this file.

□ The second parallel effort consists of sending the contract to the proposal department for project number assignment, updating of the project estimate, and preparation of the project management (PM) instructions. The updated project estimate is approved by the general manager, sales manager, and manager of engineering prior to transfer of responsibility from sales to project management.

□ If a project management (PM) instructions meeting is necessary, the proposals department should have completed the PM instructions for presentation to the manager of engineering before the meeting. This meeting may not be required, depending on the size of the project and priorities established by corporate management. The PM package may be given directly to the manager of engineering. Regardless, the appropriate transmittal form (Form B-5 in Appendix B) should be used to transmit the PM instructions to the manager of engineering. The PM instructions are accepted by the manager of engineering by signature on the transmittal form.

□ The proposals department retains a copy of the completed PM instructions in order to effectively carry out the control budget verification, shown in Figure 4-5. *This verification is the single most critical element for project success;* therefore, it has been highlighted in Figure 4-5.

Project Management (PM) Instructions

The PM instructions represent a transfer of project responsibility from the sales function to the project management function. Therefore, the instructions should be detailed and complete. As a minimum, the instructions should contain the following, as applicable:

□ Transmittal form.
□ Project proposal (updated to reflect the latest sale agreements).
□ Completed contract.

☐ Applicable customer specifications.
☐ Other Pertinent Company/Customer Communications.
☐ Initial control budget approved by the general manager, sales manager, and manager of engineering (prepared in accordance with the general chart of accounts).

The PM instructions should be bound such that they are contained in some type of "manual" or set of manuals. Loose paper, other than the transmittal form, should be avoided because this documentation manual(s) will be the project baseline for the duration of the project.

Initial Control Budget

As part of the PM instructions, the initial control budget should be prepared in accordance with the updated project estimate and general chart of accounts. The initial control budget should be prepared according to, and including all tertiary accounts. If necessary, the proposal department may request that engineering department personnel assist in preparing this initial control budget. However, the total responsibility for budget adequacy and accuracy belongs to the proposals department. Since the initial control budget is the most important part of the PM instructions, no information or project responsibility should be transferred from sales to project management until the initial control budget is completed and approved. For ease of reference, evolution of the initial control budget is shown in Figure 4-7.

Project Management Function

Project management for the example engineering and construction company reports to an intermediate management level (manager of engineering) which, in turn, reports to the general manager (Figure 4-1). Consequently, the manager of engineering has the ultimate responsibility for performance on all projects. However, each project manager should be individually responsible for his respective project(s). In some companies, project engineers perform both project management and project engineering functions. Industry defines the project management function as primarily involving commercial, financial, and management tasks, while the project engineer usually performs primarily technical tasks.

Project cost control basically involves control of two areas of expenditures in accordance with the project scope of work—manpower and material. Manpower is the more difficult to control since it accumulates over the duration of a project, thus requiring experience in time planning on the part of every employee. Lack of experience, foresight, and/ or poor judgment may go undetected until the manpower budget is exhausted, unless there is a constant comparison of manpower expenditure to project progress. One subtle budget culprit is schedule slippage. With each schedule milestone missed, required project manpower increases, since employees are not typically removed from the project, but instead remain on the project for a longer time. This is discussed in greater detail in Chapter 6. Material expenditures tend to be easier to control, since each occurs with a relatively clear definition of content and cost.

Since project management interfaces with all corporate departments, the work flow paths depicted in Figures 4-4 through 4-6 are not intended to show work flow by function or department, but instead the overall picture of project management work flow. Figure 4-4 depicts the overall project cost control work flow concept, with references to Figures 4-5 and 4-6. The following section describes this work flow. However, to facilitate use of this material, subsequent subsections are identified by project function (e.g., department) describing the cost control responsibility each has in the project management phase of a project.

Project Control Work Flow

The project cost control work flow basically consists of the following steps:

☐ Gathering project information.
☐ Consolidating that information in one reporting system.
☐ Providing forecasts and completion percentages based on current information.
☐ Publishing and distributing this information to corporate management.
☐ Using this information to direct future project cost control activities.

This basic work flow path, depicted in Figure 4-4, is a direct path beginning with submittal of manpower and material data, and culminating in distribution of the monthly project cost and progress report. Within this work flow path, purchasing (Figure 4-5) and the customer change order (Figure 4-6) exist as independent work flow paths. These independent paths are discussed in the following subsections.

Purchasing Work Flow. The purchasing function is the most complicated of any of the work flow paths (Figure 4-5). It contains critical decision points for determining if a project item or task is over or under the control budget value. This occurs as a result of comparing control budget information (provided by the proposal department) to pricing information (provided by the purchasing department). *The continuous involvement of two departments to make this comparison may be controversial; however, it is critical to project success.* If a project item or task is expected to overrun, the flow path requires preparation of a project overrun request and appropriate management approval. Management may require restructuring of the material requisition or vendor rebid instead of approving the overrun. One approval level value (A) must be established by corporate management. Value A is the purchase order approval level for the purchasing agent. Intermediate department management levels for purchase order approval may be established as appropriate.

Customer Change Order Work Flow. The customer change order effort (Figure 4-6) is another direct flow path with the change order initiated by either the project manager, project engineer, or the construction supervisor. The project manager should prepare the change order scope definition and coordinate department contributions for design and costing/pricing. For all change orders the proposal function should prepare cost estimates and determine pricing. The project manager will approve final pricing, obtain the appropriate management approval for the change order and present the change order to the customer for approval and funding. Once the change order is approved, it is distributed by the project manager.

Three approval level values (B, C, and D) should be established for customer change orders. Level B is a value below which a change order can be prepared, approved by the customer, and implemented by the construction supervisor independent of project management. Level C is the value of a change order that can be approved by the project manager. Level D is the value of a change order that can be approved by the manager of engineering, and above which must be approved by the general manager. Once a change order is approved by both project management and the customer, changes to the vendor scope of work to incorporate the change order should follow the purchasing work flow path described in Figure 4-5.

Engineering Department Project Cost Control Responsibility

Since all project management administratively reports to the manager of engineering, the engineering department is totally responsible for all aspects of project execution (after the sale) and, therefore, project cost control. Each department may have established administrative procedures within which each project manager must work, but the completion of all project work by any department is the responsibility (as relates to project cost control) of the project manager.

Figure 4-4 depicts the project manager's work flow responsibility. Figures 4-5 and 4-6 are referenced in Figure 4-4, but have their own work flow paths. The following describes the project cost control responsibility of major project participants within the engineering department:

Manager of Engineering

☐ Approves and presents to accounting in a timely manner (usually the first and sixteenth day of each month) engineering semi-monthly time sheets (Form B-13 in Appendix B) for all applied personnel.

☐ Reviews the monthly project cost and progress report set (Forms B-15 through 21 in Appendix B) for each project and provides any necessary assistance to each project manager.

Project Manager

One important activity of the project manager not depicted on the work flow path is the responsibility of collecting and distributing accurate minutes for all project meetings. This should be done using the respective minutes of meeting form (Form B-14 in Appendix B), which identifies personnel responsible for completing tasks within agreed to dates. The project manager's responsibilities also include:

☐ Preparation and distribution of the monthly project cost and progress report (the primary responsibility), which reflects current information (Figure 4-4). The content and distribution of this report are described in Chapter 7. The project manager should review all monthly project cost and progress report data each month and enter or update all cost forecast, planned complete, and actual complete values.

☐ Collection of data for and supervision of initial development and updating of the project schedule (Figure 4-4). Information for developing this schedule should be provided by the project engineer (using the equipment status report, Form B-11) and the chief draftsman (using the drawing list and status report, Form B-10) on the first working day of each month.

☐ Initiation of material requisitions (MR) (Form B-6) and completion of technical bid evaluations, as required (Figure 4-4).

☐ Preparation of all project overrun requests (Figure 4-5), using the respective form (Form B-12), with justification(s) and alternative(s).

☐ Initiation of customer change orders (Form B-9) as required with scope definition (Figure 4-6).

☐ Coordination of customer change order preparation (design and pricing) by various departments and approves final pricing (Figure 4-6).
☐ Presentation of the completed change order to the customer for funding approval (Figure 4-6).
☐ Distribution for the approved customer change order (Figure 4-6).

Project Engineer

☐ Prepares material requisitions (MR) and customer change orders, as required.
☐ Prepares technical bid evaluations as required, using the preferred subcontractor/vendor transmittal form (Form B-7).
☐ Prepares the equipment status report on the first working day of each month and provides same to the project manager.
☐ Participates in and supervises project design.

Chief Draftsman

☐ Presents approved drafting applied personnel semi-monthly time sheets to accounting in a timely manner (usually by the first and sixteenth day of each month) for processing.
☐ Prepares on the first working day of each month the drawing list and status report for each project, and provides same to the project manager.

Proposal Department Project Cost Control Responsibility

☐ Develop and transmit to the engineering department, using the appropriate form (Form B-5), the PM instructions (including the initial control budget).
☐ Provide budget value verification for each material requisition (MR) on each project. All MR's should be prepared by the engineering department, presented to the proposal department for budget verification and purchase recommendations and then presented to purchasing for inquiry (Figure 4-5). The proposal department representative signs each MR after entering or verifying budget values.
☐ Assist the project manager by providing a cost estimating and pricing service for customer change orders (Figure 4-6).

Purchasing Department Project Cost Control Responsibility

☐ Provide assistance to the proposal department in preparing project proposals.

☐ Provide purchase order data to accounting for processing.

☐ Prepare material and services inquiries for all projects. Request and receive vendor bids.

☐ Prepare a commercial bid evaluation for each material requisition (MR) response and forward same to the engineering department with the three lowest acceptable bids for technical evaluation.

☐ Determine, from budget verification values on the material requisition and prices received on vendor quotations (the one selected by engineering department), if a current control budget item or task may be overrun. If purchase of the item or service to complete a task would result in an overrun, return the MR to the project manager and take no further action. If this purchase would not cause an overrun, obtain the appropriate purchase approval (in accordance with the level of expenditure) and purchase the item or service.

Accounting Department Project Cost Control Responsibility

☐ Verify vendor invoices against purchase orders (Form B-8) before seeking payment approval. This includes verification of contractor semi-monthly time sheets against invoices. Payment approval may use a voucher system.

☐ Compile all current manpower and purchased material data in a timely manner for preparation of the monthly project cost and progress report. Semi-monthly time sheets and purchase order data should be provided to the accounting department by the first working day of each month.

☐ Collect all data, integrate and publish the monthly project cost and progress report for each project. The contents of these reports are described in Chapter 7. After each report is compiled, it should be presented to the respective project manager for entry of cost forecast, planned completion, and actual completion values. Reports for each project should be distributed (as described in Chapter 7) in a timely manner.

Summary

This chapter has primarily addressed, through example, the work flow path fundamentals as they may relate to a typical engineering and construction company. This involved the two primary areas of project cost control functional participation—sales and project management. The single most important aspect is the constant involvement (as shown in Figure 4-5) of the sales function (those who initiate the project) in the project management phase of the project through to completion. Implementation of this feature in existing company work flow paths is often controversial. However, the check and balance provided by this feature is the fundamental cause of the cost convergence discussed in Chapter 2 and shown in Figure 2-3.

The same fundamental work flow path concepts presented for the example engineering and construction company in this chapter may be used for projects completed by a manufacturing or operating company. The department or functional area names may differ, but the basic work flow will be similar.

To assist the reader in applying the fundamentals presented in this chapter, Appendix C contains an example problem that utilizes the RIICH technique discussed in Chapter 2 and the work flow path fundamentals presented in this chapter.

Chapter 5
The Numbering Systems' System

A project cost control program may be beset by many stumbling blocks, but none so devastating as entrenched numbering systems. Once a departmental numbering system has been in use for some time, employees resist changing the system to accommodate an intercompany project cost control program. Such unstated issues as pride of authorship and retraining subtly contribute to this resistance to change. How does this problem evolve?

When a new company begins business, numbering systems are low on management's priority list. But as the company grows, what initially seemed to be a simple undertaking of numbering documentation for reference becomes an overwhelming maze of dehumanizing numbers that plague every daily effort. With a little guidance in this area, most reference numbers or numbering systems used by various departments or groups can be shorter and meaningfully interrelated. This is known as the "numbering systems' system," and serves to control the creation of departmental numbering subsystems.

Example Numbering Systems

Each group or department within a growing company normally establishes some paperwork numbering system for itself. The following examples represent the type and quantity of numbering systems that typically evolve or exist in an engineering and construction company; X represents a numerical identifier (e.g., 1 though 9), while A represents an alpha identifier (e.g., A through Z).

Accounting Department

Corporate Chart of Accounts. Developed by a parent corporation, this system becomes the new company requirement for financial reporting. A preconceived corporate chart of accounts is used by an independent company only if the new controller arrives with a chart of accounts under his arm. Once the first year's taxes are submitted, changing a corporate chart of accounts is nearly impossible, since long-term account consistency for the Internal Revenue Service is important.

Check Numbering System. This system is established by the accounting department or a banking institution. It is usually sequential, starting with a company identifying prefix:

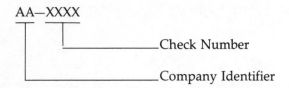

AA—XXXX

—————————Check Number

—————————Company Identifier

Invoice Numbering System. Established by the department, this usually has a project or contract number identifier:

AAA—XXXX—XX—XXXX

—————————Invoice Number

—————————Change Order Number

—————————Project Number

—————————Customer Identifier

Voucher Numbering System. This system is established by the department to identify the related purchase order number to the approved vendor invoice number and the company check number:

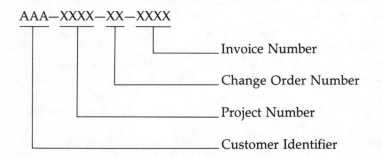

AAA—XXX—XXXX ———————Voucher Number

—————————Project Number

—————————Customer Identifier

Employee Numbering System. The department establishes this system to identify individual employees:

XX—XXX

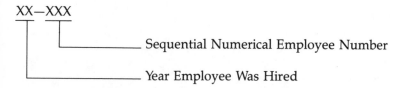

Sequential Numerical Employee Number

Year Employee Was Hired

Employee Classification Numbering System. This system helps the department identify hourly charge rates:

XX—A

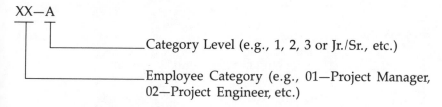

Category Level (e.g., 1, 2, 3 or Jr./Sr., etc.)

Employee Category (e.g., 01—Project Manager, 02—Project Engineer, etc.)

Work Code Numbering System. The department identifies categories of work performed with this system. Although identified with the accounting department, this numbering system is used by all employees:

XX

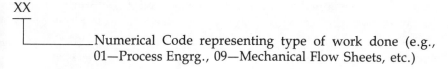

Numerical Code representing type of work done (e.g., 01—Process Engrg., 09—Mechanical Flow Sheets, etc.)

Sales Department

General Chart of Accounts. The sales department uses this system to numerically identify each item or task included in each project. Although identified with the sales department, the general chart of accounts is used by every company employee in some manner. The following numbering example is detailed in Appendix A:

X.X—XX XX

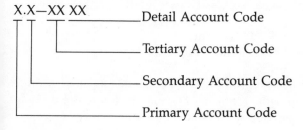

Detail Account Code

Tertiary Account Code

Secondary Account Code

Primary Account Code

Proposal Numbering System. This system is used by the sales department to identify proposal effort and number of proposals:

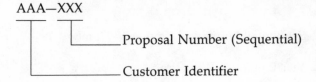

AAA—XXX

Proposal Number (Sequential)

Customer Identifier

Project Numbering System. The department uses this system to identify each project sold:

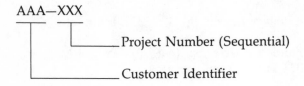

AAA—XXX

Project Number (Sequential)

Customer Identifier

Customer Contract Numbering System. This is the customer's system for identifying a project contract. This numbering scheme, because it has been developed by a second company, could conform to one of many formats and could be lengthy. Therefore, no example is given here.

Engineering Department

General Specification Numbering System. The engineering department uses this system to identify equipment specifications:

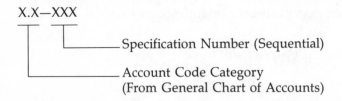

X.X—XXX

Specification Number (Sequential)

Account Code Category
(From General Chart of Accounts)

Material Requisition (MR) Numbering System. Established by the department to identify material requisition submittals to the purchasing department. Each number usually contains a project number identifier:

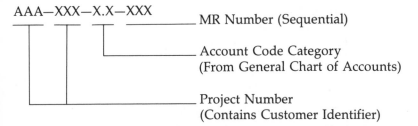

AAA–XXX–X.X–XXX
— MR Number (Sequential)

— Account Code Category
(From General Chart of Accounts)

— Project Number
(Contains Customer Identifier)

Customer Change Order Numbering System. The engineering department uses this system to identify submitted and approved customer change orders:

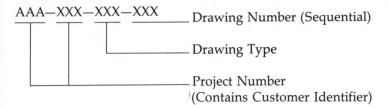

AAA–XXX–XXX
— Customer Change Order Number (Sequential)

— Project Number (Contains Customer Identifier)

Drawing Numbering System. This system is used by the department to identify project drawings. Each number usually contains a project number identifier:

AAA–XXX–XXX–XXX
— Drawing Number (Sequential)

— Drawing Type

— Project Number
(Contains Customer Identifier)

Mechanical Equipment Numbering System. Established by the department to identify major and minor project equipment, these numbers are usually located on the project drawings and project equipment status report:

AAA–XXX
— Equipment Number (Sequential)

— Equipment Category

Line Numbering System. Established by the department to identify major piping runs, these numbers are usually located on the project drawings and line list:

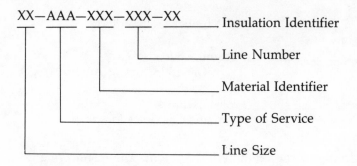

Insulation Identifier

Line Number

Material Identifier

Type of Service

Line Size

Instrument Numbering System. Established by the department to identify individual instruments, these numbers are usually located on the project drawings and the instrument list:

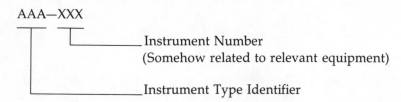

Instrument Number
(Somehow related to relevant equipment)

Instrument Type Identifier

Instrument Loop Numbering System. Established by the department to identify individual instrument loops, these numbers are usually located on the instrument loop drawings and the instrument loop list:

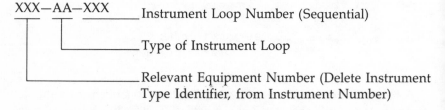

Instrument Loop Number (Sequential)

Type of Instrument Loop

Relevant Equipment Number (Delete Instrument Type Identifier, from Instrument Number)

Electrical Equipment Numbering System. Established by the department to identify electrical equipment, these numbers are usually located on the electrical layout drawings and the electrical equipment list:

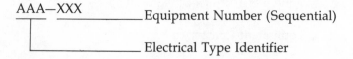

Equipment Number (Sequential)

Electrical Type Identifier

Electrical Cable Numbering System. This system is used by the engineering department to identify electrical wiring. These numbers are usually located on the electrical layout drawings and the cable list:

```
AA–XX–XX                    Cable Number (Sequential)

                            Number of Wire Pair Identifier

                            Cable Type
```

Purchasing Department

Request for Quotation (RFQ) Numbering System. The purchasing department uses this system to identify RFQ's. These numbers usually contain a project identifier:

```
AAA–XXX–X.X–XXX      RFQ Number (Sequential)

                     Account Code Category (From General
                     Chart of Accounts)

                     Project Number (Contains Customer
                     Identifier)
```

Purchase Order (PO) Numbering System. Established by the department to identify individual purchase orders, these numbers usually contain a project identifier:

```
AAA–XXX–X.X–XXX      PO Number (Sequential)

                     Account Code Category
                     (From General Chart of Accounts)

                     Project Number (Contains
                     Customer Identifier)
```

Subcontract Numbering System. The department uses this system to identify each subcontract:

```
AAA–XXX–X.X–XXX      Subcontract Number (Sequential)

                     Account Code Category (From General
                     Chart of Accounts)

                     Project Number (Contains
                     Customer Identifier)
```

Vendor/Subcontractor Numbering System. The department numerically identifies vendors or subcontractors with this system:

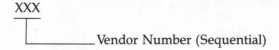

XXX

‾‾‾‾‾‾‾‾‾‾‾ Vendor Number (Sequential)

Administration

Letter Numbering System. Established by management to identify individual letters, these numbers usually contain a project or department identifier:

AAA—XXX—XXX—XXX

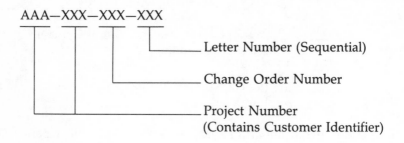

‾‾‾‾‾‾‾‾‾‾‾ Letter Number (Sequential)

‾‾‾‾‾‾‾‾‾‾‾ Change Order Number

‾‾‾‾‾‾‾‾‾‾‾ Project Number
(Contains Customer Identifier)

Meeting Numbering System. Management identifies project meetings with these numbers, which usually contain a project identifier and appear on minutes of meetings:

AAA—XXX—AA—XXX

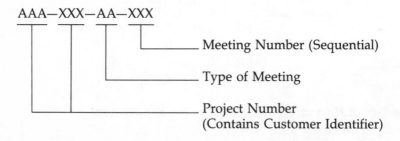

‾‾‾‾‾‾‾‾‾‾‾ Meeting Number (Sequential)

‾‾‾‾‾‾‾‾‾‾‾ Type of Meeting

‾‾‾‾‾‾‾‾‾‾‾ Project Number
(Contains Customer Identifier)

The previous examples represent 27 different numbering systems typically used by companies. Therefore, in some companies there is a sense of urgency to be the first to begin using a group or departmental numbering system in the belief that company employees will continue to use the first numbering system reduced to practice. Consequently, simultaneous, autonomous creation of departmental numbering systems begins and continues amid management's cry of "keep it simple."

Number Relationships and Optimization

To control costs, departments must not operate completely autonomously. Therefore, departmental numbering systems must also not be created autonomously. If specific number relationships are established in the beginning, numbers will be easier to identify, interpret, and remember.

Number System Relationships

The following number relationships provide a suggested guide to help keep things simple:

Interdepartmental Common Identifiers	Contained in the
☐ Project number or customer contract number	Invoice number MR number Change order number Drawing number RFQ number PO number Subcontract number Letter number Meeting number
☐ General chart of accounts	Accounting—corporate chart of accounts

Intradepartmental Common Identifiers	Relationships
☐ Accounting	None
☐ Sales Proposal number	Identical to the project number
☐ Engineering Mechanical equipment number Instrument equipment number Electrical equipment number Instrument number	All made part of the same interrelated numbering system
☐ Purchasing Request for quotation number	Identical to the PO or subcontract number
☐ Administration	None

Number System Optimization

To optimize specific number systems, the following suggestions are offered:

Departmental Identifier	Potential Optimizations
☐ **Accounting**	
Corporate chart of accounts	An expansion of the general chart of accounts
Employee number	Employee Social Security Number
Work code number	Identified by work category only; do not attempt to identify by drawing specification, etc.
☐ **Sales**	
Proposal number	Identical to the project number
Project number	As short as possible due to company wide use and because it becomes a part of many other numbers.
☐ **Engineering**	
Material request number	Purchasing—Identical to the PO or subcontract number
Line number	Identifies associated piece(s) of major mechanical equipment
Instrument equipment number	Identifies associated piece(s) of major mechanical or electrical equipment
Instrument loop number	Identifies associated piece(s) of major mechanical or electrical equipment
☐ **Purchasing**	
Vendor/subcontractor number	Vendor/subcontractor tax identification number
☐ **Administration**	None

Creating the Numbering Systems' System

It is obvious from the previous sections that a company numbering system guideline is necessary in any company simply due to the potential variations of the many number identifiers needed. Consequently, each departmental numbering system must become a subsystem of the company numbering system (i.e., the numbering systems' system). To develop such a system, follow these three steps:

Step 1—List all existing numbering subsystems, as illustrated in the examples at the beginning of this chapter.

Step 2—Establish necessary numbering subsystem interrelationships, as illustrated in "Number Relationships and Optimization." From a long-term standpoint, it is wise to disallow alpha identification of number identifiers (e.g., project number) that have an interdepartmental use. Use of alpha identifiers may complicate future project cost control system computerization, as discussed in Chapter 7.

Step 3—Develop a written numbering guideline showing the department number subsystem relationship to the corporate numbering system. All department managers should be involved in the development and approval of such a guideline.

Based on the discussion and examples presented in the previous sections, the following guidelines for the numbering systems' system emerge. The first typical interdepartmental identifier is the project number. Other interdepartmental identifiers may be peculiar to specific companies. Consequently, one guideline is to keep the project number as short and simple as possible to make it easy to use and integrate with other numbers. A four-digit sequential number is the simplest. A second guideline is to integrate the general and corporate charts of accounts. Keeping up with two charts of accounts is time consuming and wasteful.

It must be emphasized that these two guidelines were most easily derived from the discussion and examples presented. Other guidelines specific to individual companies may emerge when the three-step procedure is used to develop a numbering systems' system. Based on the guidelines that emerge from analyzing numbering subsystems, such as those examples previously cited and covered by Step 1, the remaining departmental numbering subsystem details can then be developed, as covered by Steps 2 and 3.

Since the success of a project cost control program depends primarily upon accurate and efficient communication between groups or departments, any numbering system or subsystem eventually has some influence. Consequently, one long-term company effort should be planning of corporate numbering systems, realizing that this will improve clarity of communications. The result will always be improved project cost control.

Customer Numbering System Integration

Thus far, this chapter has focused on the numbering system and subsystems of an engineering and construction company. One additional numbering system problem needs some discussion—customer numbering system integration. This area deals with any necessary integration of the customer and the engineering and construction company's numbering systems. Of course, this problem is unique to the engineering and construction company, and is typically not encountered by manufacturing or operating companies, since in a contracting relationship manufacturing and operating companies are the customers.

The engineering and construction company's customer has numbering systems it requires the engineering and construction company to use in completing a project under contract. The most common example of this requirement is when the contractual arrangement requires that all equipment and material be purchased by the customer using the customer's purchase order procedure and forms. In this instance, the engineering and construction company typically carries out all inquiry activity, completes the customer's purchase order forms and submits them to the customer for approval and processing. This means the purchase order number must be compatible with both the customer's purchase order numbering system and the engineering and construction company's project numbering system. The normal tendency in solving this problem is to add numeric and/or alphanumeric codes to the end of the customer's purchase order number to establish any necessary engineering and construction company identification. This usually results in an extremely long purchase order number that is incompatible with the customer's numbering system and any computer used for data handling. An example purchase order number that can result from such a situation is as follows:

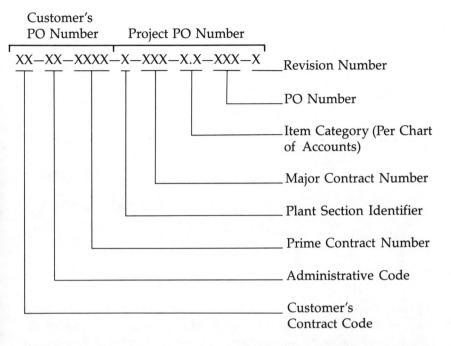

To "keep it simple" and avoid massive number handling problems, the solution here is for the customer to adopt the engineering and construction company's purchase order numbering system on a one-project basis in order to retain the continuity and interrelationship of the engineering and construction company's numbering systems' system. This approach avoids additional project costs incurred as a result of being required to re-evaluate and reoptimize the engineering and construction company's numbering system utilizing various customer numbering subsystems.

However, if the customer requires that the engineering and construction company use one or more of the customer's numbering subsystems, one possible solution would be to suppress printing (when using a computer) of some portions of the purchase order number on the purchase order listing in order to reduce the number dilemma. Only those portions of the purchase order number relevant to the company receiving the listing are printed on that company's purchase order listing. However, in most cases even this provides only a limited solution to such a problem, since this requires extensive use of computer capacity for data handling. Typically, customer numbering system integration is handled on a case-by-case basis.

Chapter 6
Project Schedule
and Cost Considerations

Management should be familiar with those schedule and cost considerations that contribute to the success of any project cost control program. These considerations involve only the fundamentals of planning, scheduling, estimating, and cost control. Execution details of these activities should be delegated to appropriate line or staff personnel. This chapter, therefore, presents only those project schedule and cost fundamentals of interest to management in making project cost control decisions.

Several project cost control program guidelines should be considered when preparing project schedules and estimates. The program should begin with proposal development, which includes the proposal schedule and project estimate. This early cost control planning improves the communication between sales and project management, as discussed in Chapter 2. Scheduling considerations are discussed first, since, during preparation of the proposal, it is important to develop the proposal schedule before or simultaneously with the project estimate. Consequently, the following discussion is presented in this same sequence, and assumes that the reader is familiar with scheduling and estimating methods, even though he may not have participated in their detail development. Selected references, which detail scheduling and estimating methods, are presented at the end of this chapter.

Project Schedule Considerations

The phrase "time is money" is often echoed by many with good intention, but few actually realize and utilize the true meaning of this phrase.

Since the cost of project time during the later phase of a project (e.g., construction phase) is far greater than during the initial phase (e.g., design phase), it is very important to project cost success to have thorough planning at the start. Some industry analysts have estimated the completion/start project time-cost ratio can be as large as 300 to 1. This ratio indicates that time spent on a project during the later phase is approximately 300 times more costly than time spent in the initial phases. This is primarily due to the increasing number of personnel involved with the project as it progresses. Therefore, any change in the later phases of a project impacts a greater number of personnel and a greater number of hardware characteristics that may have already been designed, manufactured, and/or fabricated. Project changes, which include schedule slippage, are directly affected by this ratio. To rush a project in the initial phase (i.e., proceed without comprehensive, thorough planning) may result in extra costs due to required rework. However, industry historical results have generally indicated that project delays resulting from over-planning prior to project start are more costly. Therefore, an equitable balance in initial planning and a healthy initial project inertia resulting from a quick start will achieve optimum project cost results.

Several project planning and scheduling techniques have been developed. Some are simple, such as the bar chart, and have been in use for the last century. While the more sophisticated methods (e.g., arrow diagram and PERT) were developed in the 1950s as a result of the advent of larger more sophisticated industrial projects and acceptance of computers. Consequently, present-day management has several planning and scheduling techniques from which to choose. This, of course, in itself is a problem in that each technique has an optimum application and it is possible to waste much of the project budget selecting and applying an inappropriate technique. This situation is further complicated since later techniques, in many cases, are modifications of earlier techniques. Therefore, differences, advantages, and/or appropriate applications may not be obvious. Consequently, selecting the optimum method without a thorough background in scheduling is difficult. A last complicating factor is the illusion by some in the industry that critical path techniques (e.g., the CPM technique) are universally optimum for many types of projects and that project size does not influence the decision to select these techniques.

Management should generally understand the fundamentals, advantages/disadvantages, and applications of each planning and scheduling technique. To this end, Table 6–1 and the following glossary of planning/scheduling terms and techniques are presented.

The glossary offers fundamental definitions of various techniques. More detailed information can be found in the references listed at the end of this chapter. Table 6–1 compares these techniques in the sequence they evolved and provides an example optimum application guideline for each. The techniques addressed here (with specific examples presented in Figure 6-2) are the fundamental planning/scheduling techniques. Other technique variations such as PERT/Cost, Q-GERT, P-GERT, and R-GERT are available for use, but have typically been developed to emphasize a particular feature or enhance a shortcoming of one of the fundamental techniques.

Table 6-1
Comparison of Planning/Scheduling Techniques

Suggested Plan/Schedule Techniques	Primary Characteristics	Advantages/ Disadvantages	Example Optimum Application
Bar chart	Use of graphically illustrated bars to control task time	☐ Project planning & scheduling and progress are graphically shown together making a clear, simple account of the project. ☐ Cannot show sufficient detail on long duration tasks to avoid schedule slippage ☐ Task dependency relationships cannot be clearly shown ☐ Manually updated	Repetitive type projects with low engineering contents or smaller, one-of-a-kind projects
Arrow diagram (activity-on-arrows)	Use of arrows to represent project tasks (activities) arranged so as to	☐ Project planning may be separate from scheduling un-	Production planning or other applications where clarity of conflict-

Suggested Plan/Schedule Techniques	Table 6-1 continued Primary Characteristics	Advantages/ Disadvantages	Example Optimum Application
	show task inter-dependency	less the net-work is illus-trated on a time scale	ing requirements is of primary im-portance; other projects of an in-termediate size
		☐ Greater proj-ect task detail available than bar chart	
		☐ Clearly shows task interde-pendency	
		☐ Changes in the duration of one task may require move-ment of fol-lowing tasks on a time scale, thereby causing signifi-cant redraw-ing time	
		☐ Simpler than the prece-dence diagram	
Node diagram (activity-on-nodes)	Use of nodes to represent project tasks intercon-nected by ar-rows; reverse of the arrow dia-gram	☐ Eliminates the need for dummy ar-rows in the ar-row diagram to correct false dependencies	Production plan-ning or other ap-plications where clarity of conflict-ing requirements is of primary im-portance; consid-ered secondary in preference to the arrow dia-gram except when used on construction type projects where many activities are concurrent.
		☐ More efficient & compact than the arrow diagram & easier to learn	
		☐ More involved computational procedure than arrow di-agram	
Precedence dia-gram (Extension	Extension of the node diagram;	☐ Same as node diagram	Production plan-ning or other ap-

(Table continued on next page)

Table 6-1 continued

Suggested Plan/Schedule Techniques	Primary Characteristics	Advantages/ Disadvantages	Example Optimum Application
of Activity-on-Nodes or Node Diagram)	Addition of elements such as lead/lag times	☐ Modifications provide greater flexibility and use than the node diagram	plications where clarity of conflicting requirements is of primary importance; considered secondary in preference to the arrow diagram
Project evaluation and review technique (PERT)	Depiction of project event sequence and interdependency, allowing determination of probability of meeting schedule	☐ Requires establishing project objectives and a method for determining how to achieve these reducing the risk of oversights ☐ Provides clear documentation for communicating project plans & progress ☐ Establishes interim objectives ☐ Emphasizes the concept of management by exception ☐ Allows determination of numerical probabilities associated with variances in project completion times	Applied research and development projects or other projects comprised primarily of activities whose duration times are subject to considerable variation
Critical path method (CPM)	Depiction of project event sequence and interdependency allowing deter-	☐ Similar to those listed for PERT since both are considered critical	Design and construction projects and maintenance programs

Table 6-1 continued

Suggested Plan/Schedule Techniques	Primary Characteristics	Advantages/ Disadvantages	Example Optimum Application
	mination of project time-cost tradeoff's	path techniques □ Allows determination of project task completion times which minimize total project cost	
Graphical evaluation and review technique (GERT)	A generalized arrow diagram; incorporates techniques for network branching and looping	□ Same as arrow diagram □ Allows the evaluation of alternatives	Projects such as research which involve testing and recycle if testing results in failure; may be used for project startup where rework may be necessary

The project plan and schedule are developed in accordance with the phases of a project and in a similar manner as project costs. The logical evolution of project schedules and costs is depicted in Figure 6-1. Initial project planning and estimating may be as coarse or as detailed as time permits during the proposal development in accordance with the level of risk acceptable to management. Project schedules and budgets developed later in the project must be detailed and thorough in order to succeed in project cost control.

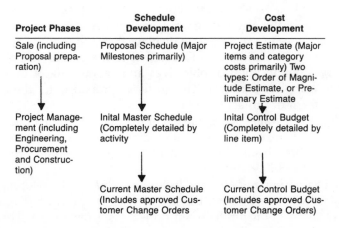

Project Phases	Schedule Development	Cost Development
Sale (including Proposal preparation)	Proposal Schedule (Major Milestones primarily)	Project Estimate (Major items and category costs primarily) Two types: Order of Magnitude Estimate, or Preliminary Estimate
Project Management (including Engineering, Procurement and Construction)	Inital Master Schedule (Completely detailed by activity	Inital Control Budget (Completely detailed by line item)
	Current Master Schedule (Includes approved Customer Change Orders	Current Control Budget (Includes approved Customer Change Orders)

Figure 6-1. Project plan/schedule and estimate/budget development.

Glossary of Scheduling Terms

Arrow Diagram (Activity-on-Arrows)—A logical network of project tasks (synonymous with activities) that uses arrows to represent the tasks (see Figure 6-2B). Sometimes network arrows will have activity descriptions and time estimates written on them. The tasks or activity arrows are connected head-to-tail in a manner such that their intersections (called nodes or events) represent task interdependencies and project events or milestones. When arrow diagrams are represented on a time scale, this is basically an extension of the bar chart.

Bar Chart—A graphically illustrated means of showing the duration of individual project tasks using a bar of a length proportional to the task duration (see Figure 6-2A). The bar is placed on a time scale that connects the start and finish dates of individual project tasks or the total project.

Critical Path Method (CPM)—Developing a project plan through the use of a logical network diagram that shows the relationships between project tasks (activities). The project duration is essentially determined by calculating the longest (critical) path through the network (see Figure 6-2D). CPM is based on a single task time value. The technique allows the determination of project task completion times that minimize total project cost.

Graphical Evaluation and Review Technique (GERT)—A generalized arrow diagram that incorporates techniques for handling network branching and looping. This allows the evaluation of alternatives in specialized applications, which include testing and recycle due to test failure.

Node Diagram (Activity-on-Nodes)—A logical network of project tasks (activities) that uses nodes to represent project tasks or activities. It is the *reverse* of the arrow diagram technique. Arrows are used to connect the nodes in a manner that displays their sequence as constrained by their interdependencies. Forerunner to the precedence diagram.

Planning—Identification of objectives and sequencing of tasks necessary to complete a project. This includes preparing for the optimum commitment of project funding.

Precedence Diagram—An extension of the node diagram or activity-on-nodes (see Figure 6-2C). Several modifications (e.g., addition of lead/lag times) have been added to the node diagram to allow greater plan/schedule flexibility and use.

Project Evaluation and Review Technique (PERT)—Developing a project plan/schedule through the use of a logical network diagram that shows the relationship between project tasks (activities). The project duration is essentially determined by calculating the longest (critical) path through the network. PERT is a critical path technique based on a system of three task time estimates and allows the development of probabilities for project completion times. Several scheduling techniques such as CPM (see Figure 6-2D) resulted from modification of the basic PERT techniques.

Scheduling—A means, in most instances graphically illustrated, of showing planned, actual, and forecast progress of a project.

A) EXAMPLE BAR CHART

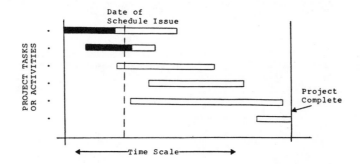

NOTES: 1) Bars are shaded to indicate status on date
        of schedule issue

B) EXAMPLE ARROW DIAGRAM (Time Scaled)

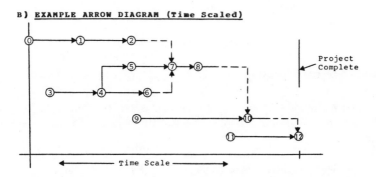

NOTES) 1) Arrows indicate project tasks or activities

        2) Nodes indicate project milestones or events

Figure 6-2. Example planning/scheduling techniques.

C) EXAMPLE PRECEDENCE DIAGRAM

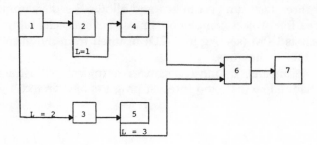

NOTES: 1) Arrows indicate precedence relationships; Lag values are
          placed on the arrows

       2) Nodes (boxes) represent project tasks or activities

D) EXAMPLE CRITICAL PATH TECHNIQUE

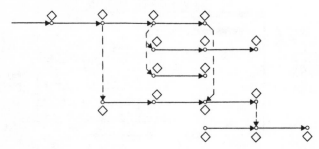

NOTES) 1) Arrows represent project tasks or activities (may be
          listed on arrows)

       2) Nodes (circles) represent project events or milestones

       3) Diamonds indicate the week or date the event is scheduled
          to occur

Figure 6-2. Continued.

Initial Project Planning

During the sale phase of any project, four fundamental documents
should be developed during proposal preparation in the following order:

1. Project scope of work (reflected in the proposal)
2. Project work plan (internal document)
3. Proposal schedule (reflected in the proposal)
4. Project estimate (internal document; pricing summary reflected in
   the proposal)

Each subsequent document is developed based on the content of the previous document. All documents should use the framework outlined by the general chart of accounts, as described in Chapter 3. Project activities (identified by account codes) on the proposal schedule should closely match those listed in the project estimates. The numbering system integration for projects, discussed in Chapter 5, should also be closely followed. Although proposal preparation time during the sale phase of any project is normally considered too short, the close coordination of these four documents and the development of as much document detail as possible will make project cost control during the project management phase easier and more effective.

The proposal schedule should not be the current "best guess"; instead, it should be developed using available historical and current data. If the proposal schedule consists of only a start and finish date, perhaps sufficient detail is not available to support tendering a proposal. Preparation of a proposal schedule using accurate data is less difficult and requires less effort than any other single task completed while preparing a proposal.

The proposal schedule should consist of a logical sequence of major activities required to complete such a project using generic designs unless the specific project has unique features. These major activities, as a minimum, should consist of the fundamental project elements (e.g., design, procurement, fabrication, construction and testing/startup). Of course, the more scheduling detail entered at this time, the easier it will be to understand the proposal schedule concept when the project is begun. For example, the major project activities may be subdivided into identifiable project work groups (e.g., equipment modules or processes). Current lead times and activity overlap must be realistically included, balancing the sales person's optimism with the project manager's caution. Example minimum proposal schedules using the bar chart or network techniques are shown in Figure 6-2. Absence of schedule detail should indicate to management that proposal planning has not been completed, or that a higher risk of schedule oversights must be accepted in tendering the proposal. The proposal schedule establishes the framework for subsequent project schedules and provides the time frame upon which the project estimate is based.

In essence, the important project schedule characteristics peculiar to initial project planning (that concern project cost control) are:

☐ Develop the proposal schedule using the framework outlined by the general chart of accounts.
☐ Proposal schedule activities should closely match those listed in the project estimate.

□ The numbering system integration discussed in Chapter 5 should be used in initial project planning.

□ Accurate, historical, and current data should be used to develop the proposal schedule.

□ As much detail as possible, considering the proposal preparation time frame, should be included in the proposal schedule.

Project Execution

The execution of a project after the sale should include two basic scheduling activities—schedule development/upkeep, and schedule analysis/control. Each of these activities is carried out using techniques somewhat standardized in most industries.

Schedule Development and Upkeep. The degree of schedule complexity depends on the type of scheduling technique used and size and complexity of the project. For every project there is a scheduling level (as in cost control) below which the cost of the scheduling activity exceeds the benefit derived. A project control budget must be capable of supporting a justifiable level of scheduling activity. One rule of thumb used by management is that the total cost of accounting, scheduling, and cost control activities applied directly to a project should range from 1% to 3% of the total project control budget. A second guideline is the "1% Rule"—project activities that consume less than 1% of their major schedule category (e.g., design and procurement) should be part of a group rather than individually tracked.

Project schedule development may necessitate only minor expansion of the proposal schedule or require the development of an extensive cascading schedule system. Such a system involves the cascading of various contractor level schedule information, as shown in Figure 6-3. Extra features, such as resource allocation, can also be added to scheduling activities. However, management should remember that schedule complexity is directly proportional to scheduling manpower costs in both the development and upkeep of project schedules. The benefits of using a more complex technique must outweigh the increased cost.

In order to maintain schedule data at current status, schedule data must be made available from a variety of sources, such as:

Project Area	Source
Design	Project engineer and chief draftsman
Procurement/ Expediting	Purchasing agent/expeditor
Fabrication	Fabrication shop or subcontractor
Construction	Field supervisor or subcontractor

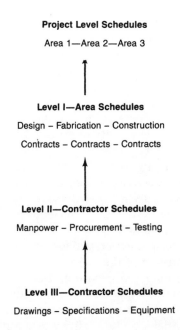

Project Level Schedules

Area 1—Area 2—Area 3

Level I—Area Schedules

Design – Fabrication – Construction

Contracts – Contracts – Contracts

Level II—Contractor Schedules

Manpower – Procurement – Testing

Level III—Contractor Schedules

Drawings – Specifications – Equipment

Figure 6-3. Cascading schedule data flow.

Example forms for design status reporting (Form B-10) and equipment status reporting (Form B-11) are available in Appendix B. Other schedule data reporting forms may need to be custom designed for each specific company.

In essence, the important project schedule characteristics peculiar to project execution (that concern project cost control) are:

☐ Do not exceed the "1% Rule" when scheduling.
☐ Keep project schedules within the framework of the proposal schedule.
☐ Financially justify use of new scheduling techniques or addition of extra schedule features before implementation.
☐ Properly designed schedule status reporting forms are important to efficient communication and may determine success or failure of schedule control activities.

Schedule Analysis/Control. Once project schedules are developed, schedule control is carried out in much the same manner as cost control. It is important to note that schedule slippage directly results in cost overruns if other portions of the budget are not available to absorb the extra cost. However, the reverse is not true (i.e., cost overruns do not directly result in schedule slippage). Schedules are analyzed to identify activities predicted to be or presently exceeding a previously planned time allocation (i.e., schedule activity overrun). The impact on the total project schedule of an activity, for example, is quantified using a critical path scheduling technique, by comparing the schedule critical path with and without showing that activity as being overrun.

If predicted individual activity overruns are each evaluated in this manner, management can avoid the "makeup syndrome." This syndrome occurs when management, upon hearing of a potential activity schedule overrun, begins to compensate for lengthening of the first activity by planning absorption of the extra time or reducing the planned schedule for another activity. Once started, this "makeup syndrome" is usually continued throughout an entire project. Consequently, schedule compression continually increases until management begins to lose credibility. If each potential schedule activity overrun is evaluated using the critical path technique, the risk of falling into the makeup syndrome is decreased. Other schedule evaluation techniques are available and covered in detail in the references listed at the end of this chapter.

Project schedule slippage is a subtle consumer of the project budget. Schedule slippage results from either proposal schedule inaccuracies, project inefficiencies, or project changes. Proposal schedule inaccuracies result from incorrect assessment of material availabilities, work priorities, or manpower availability. These incorrect assessments may involve the prime contractor, subcontractors, or equipment vendors. Project inefficiencies typically result from poor project management. Project changes reflect a change in project scope of work. Any one of these causes may result in schedule slippage. However, there are specific schedule activities not on the project schedule critical path that can absorb overrun of other schedule activities so as not to lengthen the overall project schedule. When properly analyzed most activity overruns result in some project schedule slippage. This slippage must be identified, quantified, and considered in daily project planning.

Schedule Slippage/Cost Relationships. It is sometimes difficult to verify that schedule slippage itself increases project costs. It is even more difficult to convince the customer of this. However, if the project critical path lengthens due to an activity schedule slippage, that schedule slippage has caused an increase in project costs. These project cost increases are most easily identifiable (from project management's perspective) in increased manpower costs. However, startup delays resulting in postponed production revenue are also clearly identifiable (from the customer's perspective).

Management should always endeavor to keep the project schedule within the framework of the proposal schedule, since this was the basis for the initial control budget. Proposal schedule inaccuracies must be identified early through schedule analysis, and alternatives examined that provide opportunity to effectively keep the project critical path within the proposal schedule time frame. If the project cannot be kept within the proposal schedule time frame, an increase in project manpower costs should be immediately evident in the project manager's forecasts appearing on the monthly cost and progress report. As a minimum, this predicted (forecast) manpower cost increase should include services of all project management support personnel (e.g., construction supervisor) for that time differential between the proposal schedule total project time and the predicted schedule total project time. Depending on the reason for schedule slippage, additional costs may have to be absorbed by either the contractor or customer.

Customer change orders must reflect the cost impact of schedule slippage. This cost impact is viewed from two perspectives, as described previously—that of project management and of the customer. In any event, the project critical path impact of each proposed project change must be analyzed. If the cost of schedule increases resulting from change orders is not recognized in the change order, the project manager's forecast must reflect these increases as previously outlined.

Project Cost Considerations

Project cost estimating occurs in the initial stages of every project prior to tendering a project proposal. The accuracy and thoroughness of the project estimate directly determines for an engineering and construction company the project gross profit potential after sale to the customer. This project profit consists of two components—planned sales margin and budget underruns. If the project estimate has been poorly prepared, control budget overruns can easily absorb the planned sales margin for most projects, since the planned margin usually only consists of 5 to 15% of project estimated cost. For operating companies the project does not include a planned sales margin. However, project budget underruns may contribute to company cost center performance.

Since it is not feasible from a financial or a time standpoint to design a project in detail before it is sold (thereby providing the ultimate in a project estimate), creditable historical cost data are extremely valuable to the estimator. This historical cost data are usually available from performance on past projects. However, for a new company, this source may not exist. Consequently, the estimator may need to resort to industry published estimating data. If historical cost data are available, it should exist in a framework structured by the company general chart of accounts. This should make the estimator's job easier, since the initial project estimate, like the proposal schedule discussed earlier in this chapter, establishes the framework within which the project must be completed.

The project estimate and control budget evolve in the same manner as the project schedule. That is, according to the project phases, as depicted in Figure 6-1.

Initial Project Planning

During the sale phase of any project, the four fundamental documents as stated earlier are developed—project scope of work, project work plan, proposal schedule, and project estimate. The project estimate development proceeds simultaneously with the other three efforts, but is completed last because project details presented in the other three documents must be covered by the estimate. Similar project cost control program considerations are as important with project estimate preparation as with proposal schedule preparation.

The two basic elements of any estimate are manpower and materials. Material costs are somewhat easier to estimate, since they are constant within a specified time frame. However, manpower estimates are influenced by an estimator's insight regarding work efficiency and interruptions. The cost impact of these two considerations will change not only as a function of time, but also in accordance with geographical location and political climate. An additional consideration may be currency exchange rate, if project costs are paid in a foreign currency and converted to domestic currency. These considerations also provide additional rationale for keeping a project on schedule since their involvement tends to add complication.

The estimator should prepare the project estimate within the framework established by the company general chart of accounts, as shown in Appendix A. The project estimate should be as detailed as possible, without delaying preparation and presentation of the proposal. Since the project estimate will eventually, after the sale, evolve into the initial control budget, the estimate should be structured in the appropriate format at the earliest possible convenience. The four example project cost control forms (Forms B-1 through B-4 in Appendix B)—project cost summary; project detail estimate of project management and engineering/design services; project detail estimate of personnel direct charges; and project detail estimate of purchased equipment, material, and subcontracts—were developed for this purpose. If forms with these same basic elements are used for the project estimate, transition to the initial control budget will be easier.

Project estimates are typically prepared as an order of magnitude estimate or a preliminary estimate, depending on the proposal requirements. The order of magnitude estimate is usually based on a conceptual definition of project design and scope of work. The preliminary estimate is based on design specifications and a definite scope of work. Depending on the circumstances, either type of estimate may evolve directly into the project estimate, which is detailed in accordance with the company general chart of accounts. The project estimate, after project sale, evolves into the initial control budget, as illustrated in Figure 6-1. It should be clear that the more cost definition included at the proposal phase, the easier the evolution to initial control budget and the higher the probability for maintaining planned sales margins and/or project budgets. Usually, if an order of magnitude estimate is used to sell a project, large contingency costs are included to cover estimate oversights. These contingency values are grouped into a single contingency value and allocated later when the initial control budget is prepared.

The project estimate should be prepared in the same manner and logical subdivision as it is anticipated that the project will be designed and constructed. For example, if it is intended that the project construction be subcontracted by type of craft (e.g., concrete, piping, electrical), then the project estimate should be subdivided in exactly this same manner. It may be an unaffordable overkill to completely detail each project estimate prior to proposal preparation in the name of standardization (e.g., the company requires all projects to be estimated in detail) if such detail may never be needed. From another standpoint, the greater detail may provide for a change in planning (e.g., the company provides construction materials and labor rather than subcontracting) after the project is sold. In general, the project estimate should be developed and structured in the same manner as it is anticipated that the project will be built.

The important project estimate characteristics peculiar to initial project planning (that concern project cost control) are:

☐ Develop the project estimate using the framework outlined by the general chart of accounts.
☐ Project estimate line items or tasks should closely match activities presented on the proposal schedule.
☐ The numbering system integration, discussed in Chapter 5, should be used in initial project planning.

☐ Accurate historical and current data should be used to develop the project estimate.
☐ As much detail as possible, considering the proposal preparation time frame, should be included in the project estimate.
☐ Structure the project estimate in the same manner that it is anticipated that the project will be designed and built.

Project Execution

Once project design and construction begins, a solid foundation of project budget values must exist against which project expenditures are compared. Evolution of these budget values proceeds as follows. The project estimate evolves into the initial control budget after project sale. The initial control budget is never changed and becomes resident in the monthly project cost and progress report (tertiary accounts). The project budget status is kept current with the addition of approved customer change order data. The initial control budget information is continuously combined with the approved customer change order information to form the current control budget. The current control budget is the project budgetary baseline as the project work proceeds against which expenditures are authorized and project progress is compared. The mechanics of this procedure are covered in detail in Chapter 7.

In summary, the important project estimate characteristics peculiar to project execution (that concern project cost control) are:

☐ Maintain "1% rule" for controlling costs.
☐ Establish the initial control budget within the framework of the project estimate.
☐ Financially justify extra project financial analysis features before implementation.
☐ Maintain the integrity (i.e., no changes) of the initial control budget throughout the project.
☐ Properly designed cost status reporting forms are important to efficient communication and may determine the success or failure in controlling costs.

References

Since the intent of the chapter is to illustrate the innate and necessary relationships between scheduling/estimating and project cost control, the details of scheduling/estimating techniques have not been presented. In the event that the reader wishes to review or study application and details of these techniques, the following reading material is suggested:

Scheduling

Brennan, J. *Applications of Critical Path Techniques*. New York: Elsevier, 1968.

Horowitz, Joseph. *Critical Path Scheduling: Management Control Through CPM and PERT.* Melbourne, Florida: R.E. Krieger Publishing Co., 1980.

Kerzner, Harold. *Project Management: A Systems Approach to Planning, Scheduling and Controlling.* New York: Van Nostrand Reinhold, 1979.

Kaufman, A. and Desbazielle, G. *Critical Path Method.* New York: Gordon & Breach, Inc., 1969.

Martino, R. L. *Critical Path Networks.* New York: Gordon & Breach, Inc., 1968.

Moder, Joseph J., Phillips, Cecil R., and Davis, Edward W. *Project Management with CPM, PERT, and Precedence Diagramming.* New York: Van Nostrand Reinhold Company, 1983.

O'Brien, James J. *CPM in Construction Management: Project Management with CPM.* New York: McGraw Hill, 1971.

O'Brien, James J. *Scheduling Handbook.* New York: McGraw-Hill, 1969.

Schoderbeck, Peter P. and Schoderbeck, Charles G. *Management Systems*, rev. ed. Dallas, Texas: J. Wiley, 1980.

Waldron, A. James. *Applied Principles of Project Planning and Control.* Haddonfield, NJ: J. A. Waldron Enterprises, 1968.

Weist, Jerome D. and Levy, Ferdinand K. *A Management Guide with Gert-PDM, DCPM and Other Networks.* Englewood Cliffs, NJ: Prentiss-Hall Inc., 1977.

Woodgate, H.S. *Planning by Network.* New York: Van Nostrand Reinhold, 1968.

Estimating

Bent, James A. *Applied Cost and Schedule Control.* New York: Marcel Dekker, Inc., 1982.

Clark, Forrest D. and Lorenzoni, A.B. *Applied Cost Engineering.* New York: Marcel Dekker, Inc., 1978.

Humphreys, Kenneth K. and Katell, Sidney. *Basic Cost Engineering.* New York: Marcel Dekker, Inc., 1981.

Kharbanda, O. P. *Process Plant and Equipment Cost Estimation.* Solana Beach, California: Craftsman Book Company, 1979.

King, Paul A. and Moselle, Gary. *National Construction Estimator.* Carlsbad, California: Craftsman Book Company, 1984.

Means System Costs, 9th ed. Kingston, Maine: Robert Snow Means Company, Inc., 1983.

Page, John S. *Estimator's General Construction Man-Hour Manual*, 2nd ed. Houston: Gulf Publishing Company, 1983.

Page, John S. *Conceptual Cost Estimating Manual*. Houston: Gulf Publishing Company, 1984.

Stewart, Rodney D. *Cost Estimating*. New York: John Wiley and Sons, 1982.

Ward, Sol A. and Thorndike, Litchfield. *Cost Control in Design and Construction*. New York: McGraw-Hill, 1980.

Chapter 7
Data Handling, Reporting and Use: Closing the Feedback Loop

Effective project cost control is evidenced when the project manager responds to project needs as a result of a continuous comparison between project effort and project costs. The project manager acts effectively when demonstrating the following characteristics:

☐ Knows what has to be done (established by the project control budget and scope of work).
☐ Knows what has been done (established by committed data).
☐ Knows what remains to be done (established through cost forecasting).
☐ Knows how actual project progress compares to current expenditures (established by monthly cost and progress reports).
☐ Takes action to keep from overrunning the budget or takes corrective action to bring costs back in line with the budget (evidence of cost control).
☐ Checks results of corrective action (cost control follow-up).

The first four of these items involve the "cost reporting" function; the last two are examples of project cost control. Consequently, the last two steps are critical to the effectiveness of any project cost control program.

As illustrated in Figure 7-1, previous chapters dealt with creating, verifying, and accumulating cost control data. The project cost control information/decision loop should now be closed. Closing the "feedback loop" is accomplished by manipulating the project data, thereby result-

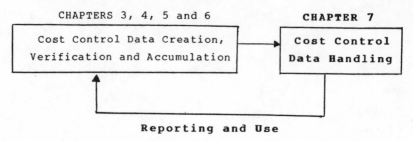

Figure 7-1. Cost control program feedback loop.

ing in a meaningful reporting system (monthly cost and progress report). Reports resulting from this system will then be distributed to management, whereupon management directs future activities of each project. This closed-loop procedure automatically results in the convergence of project expenditures with the project control budget as discussed in Chapter 2. Most of this loop was illustrated in Figure 4-4 as a direct work flow path. The practical method of closing the feedback loop is the subject of this chapter.

Project Source Data

Project source data, made available initially and updated on a periodic basis, must be collected and verified before the data handling process can begin. If the company paperwork (e.g., forms) allows for the appropriate cost control entries, as discussed in Chapter 4 and illustrated in Appendix B, all project cost control program source data will automatically be available on a continuous basis. The following identifies the sources of data needed to develop and update the monthly project reports (i.e., the monthly cost and progress report, Forms B-15 through 21 in Appendix B). The descriptions are offered in the order that they appear on the report:

☐ *Account Code, Category Description, Initial Quantity, and Initial Budget Data.* These data are taken directly from the project estimate developed by the proposals department. Control budget additions are made as a result of approved customer change orders and continuing project definition. However, once control budget data are entered, they must not be changed in order to preserve control of the project. Only data additions are permissible. An identifier (D, M, etc.) is placed behind the initial quantity value to identify the units (dollars, manhours, etc.)

☐ *Approved Customer Change Order Data.* The line item change order value identified by the account code, category/item description, and initial quantity is entered only after a change order is approved (in writing) by the customer. Approved customer change orders are received and distributed by the project manager.

☐ *Vendor/Subcontractor Name, Purchase Order Number, Committed Quantity, Committed Capital and Committed Freight, Scheduled Delivery Date Data.* These data are taken directly from issued purchase orders. Each purchased item is identified by an account code to indicate in which row the data is to be placed.

☐ *Cost Forecast, Predicted Delivery Date Data.* These values are the total anticipated cost and delivery date of a line item or task predicted by the project manager or project engineer. This prediction is updated monthly.

☐ *Planned Complete Data.* The percent (%) complete of each line item initially planned (according to the proposal schedule) at the date of report publication.

☐ *Actual Complete Data.* The actual percent (%) complete of each line item (according to the current project schedule) at the date of report publication. Suggested guidelines for determining percent complete are as follows:
- Project Management: in direct proportion to project completion
- Engineering: in direct proportion to project design completion
- Drawings: as described on the drawing list and status report form, Form B-10 in Appendix B
- Equipment and Material:
  - 45% = Material request completed
  - 50% = Inquiry issued by purchasing
  - 60% = Vendor bids received
  - 65% = Bid evaluation completed
  - 70% = Purchase order issued
  - 95% = Shipped
  - 100% = Received

☐ *Invoice Amount, Invoice Date Data.* These data should be identified as "detail" or "predicted" using an identifier (A or P). The data are updated monthly by the project manager with information from accounting regarding what invoices have been received to date and prediction of the amount and date future invoices will be received.

Data Handling

There are three basic functions associated with data handling, reporting and use:

☐ Collection and verification of project source data
☐ Data manipulation
☐ Report generation

Manpower costs for collection/verification of project source data remains constant whether or not a computer is used. For small companies, project cost control data can be economically manipulated manually to produce the required cost control reports, as discussed in Chapter 2. However, for larger companies, which started with manually manipulated data, this data manipulation may become cumbersome, requiring large manpower expenditures. Management should justify changing from manual to computer data handling based on cost savings, and improved reporting, rather than employee convenience. In some cases, the employee requesting computerized assistance can make an interesting case by describing hypothetical reporting improvements. When examined closely, however, these improvements, even with the use of a computer, require an increase in manpower rather than a decrease, and may be little used because they are needed by only a few rather than by the company.

Changing from manual to computerized data manipulation can be clearly justified with a written comparison of present manpower costs versus future manpower and computer costs accompanied by a listing of existing versus future reports, their value, and use.

Manual Data Handling

The first project cost control reporting system in a new company results from manually handling and manipulating the project source data. These reporting forms exhibited in Appendix B can be used to display source and calculated data. When only service (i.e., manpower) is the company product, manual data handling is typically the most economical technique. However, if or when equipment and materials are sold, manual data handling and manipulation become cumbersome and may justify use of a computer.

The advent and widespread acceptance of word processing equipment decreases the manpower cost of manual data handling. Since word processing equipment is justified independently (i.e., to improve handling of the typing load), it may already be available for the manual data handling function. Mathematical data manipulations (i.e., summing and averaging) are still completed manually; however, once the first report set is created and placed in word processing memory, value changes (i.e., updated project source data or adjusted sums/averages) can easily be made from the previously stored report.

If no word processing equipment is available, the mathematical data manipulation step is the same. However, each report set is then hand-written or typed each month.

Computerized Data Handling

As mentioned earlier, one common misconception is that the use of a computer program for data handling and manipulation constitutes a project cost control program. Computers are convenient and economical for handling and manipulating large quantities of data. However, their use results from an established project cost control procedure, as discussed in Chapter 4. The project cost control program consists of the project cost control procedure plus the selected data manipulation technique, either manual or computerized. There are several options for computerized data handling:

☐ Computer terminal, phone line linked to a service bureau
☐ Computer purchase
 • Hardware
  Individual dedicated unit
  Time sharing unit with common mainframe
 • Software
  Data processing only
  Data processing with word processing capability
☐ Computer lease
 • Same as computer purchase options

To determine the optimum computer system for a specific company application, each of these options should be explored in terms of equipment and software capability and cost. This investigation and evaluation should be conducted in the same manner as any other investigation of leased or purchased equipment as follows:

☐ Prepare a functional specification (addressing software requirements before hardware requirements):
 • Present use needs
 • Present desired conveniences
 • Future expansion needs
☐ Establish a vendor list and send the specification to each selected vendor.
☐ Evaluate vendor responses and select a computer.

One pitfall normally encountered is allowing an equipment supplier to determine company needs. This approach typically molds the company's computer needs to the vendor's equipment capability. This lack of objectivity typically leads to eventual inadequate or excessive computer capability.

Once the computer software and hardware selections are in progress, consideration must be given to establishing a project cost control computer program for handling data. The initial alternatives are:

☐ Use an industry available "canned" program
☐ Develop (write) an internal program

This decision is usually coupled with and made during the software and equipment selection previously described. Since project cost control computer programs do not involve iterative solutions, they may be economically developed internally, if properly handled. However, management indecision regarding what is needed can result in the internally developed program being very expensive. The fundamental scheme for computer generation of monthly cost and progress reports is shown in Figure 7-2. This flow chart scheme illustrates the simplicity of the overall computer program concept, but obviously does not show details.

Project cost control computer programs are subdivided into three sections:

☐ Project data file creation or modification
☐ Data manipulation
☐ Report generation

Depending upon type of language used, project data file creation or modification can be simple or difficult. Interactive commands will help to prompt the user. Once the project data file(s) is current and accurate, a single command normally is used to execute data manipulation and report generation. Due to the number of decision variables involved (different computer languages, various company reporting needs, etc.) guiding the reader in development of the optimum program for his company is not covered here.

Data Reporting

Following is a complete set of cost control program reports (for example forms, see Appendix B):

	Minimum Needed for Cost Control Program
A. Individual Project Reports	
1. Project data (tertiary accounts)	X
2. Management summary (secondary accounts)	X

3. Management summary (primary accounts)   X
4. Predicted project overruns   X
5. Field material report
B. Summary Reports (including all projects)
   1. Vendor summary/expediting report
   2. Project invoice schedule

    Any cost control program, as a minimum, should include the first four reports in category A in order to provide the necessary system checks and balances, as discussed in Chapter 4. Using only the first four reports would provide a minimum program. The remaining reports expand the basic cost control program into the areas of material control and account-

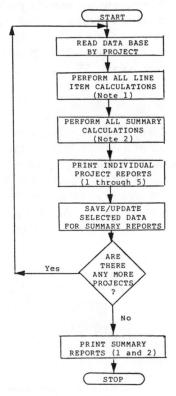

NOTES:
1) Line item calculations include calculations such as Current
   Control Budget, Total Committed, Forecast Over/Under by line
   item.

2) Summary calculations include calculations such as column
   summaries and secondary and primary column subtotals.

Figure 7-2. Fundamental computer software scheme for generation of cost control program monthly cost and progress reports.

ing. One other project report, the field material report, can be added if a project includes field fabrication or construction. This report will assist the construction supervisor in his duties.

The addition of the two reports in category B will involve considerable data manipulation, since all project data must be added together to produce these reports. Therefore, the benefit provided by category B must be carefully evaluated before adoption in the project cost control program.

For the total report set, five reports are produced per project for category A, while only two reports representing all projects are produced for category B. Sufficient copies of each report should be made to accommodate distribution.

Report categories A and B represent a complete project cost control report set. All of these reports are not necessary for every company. The reader should use this guideline report set as a starting point from which to create a set of reports that meets his company's needs without generating unused quantities of paper.

Performance Monitoring

Performance monitoring curves for each project may be plotted using the data developed as a result of a comprehensive project cost control program. These graphs reflect the relationship of cumulative project data with time. Although considered a convenience rather than a necessity in the industry, the curves clearly show the position of project cumulative cost data at any time in the project. An example of performance monitoring is shown in Figure 7-3. The detail involved in creating these

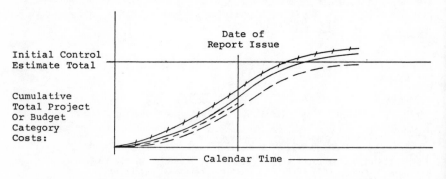

Figure 7-3. Performance monitoring curve example.

curves is not presented here. Suffice it to say that the reader may create several meaningful, informational relationships by plotting the curves he feels best emphasize specific project situations.

Here again is a situation where the benefit of a technique for data presentation that allows project analysis may be added to the project scope of work without proper justification. Certainly, preparation of performance curves from existing data should not be time consuming and costly. However, efforts such as this may get carried away so as to create many more curves for data analysis than are necessary or that are used. Care should be taken to carefully plan a justifiable project cost control program data reporting system.

Data Use

Once current data have been manipulated and displayed in report form, this information must be made available in a timely manner for management use. This process begins with appropriate report distribution and culminates with management taking action as a result of data received to redirect projects so that they are completed within the framework of the current control budget. This constitutes management closing the feedback loop.

Report Distribution

To close the feedback loop, project cost control program reports must be distributed to the appropriate members of management. All reports (which include all active projects) should be updated and distributed on the same day of each month. These reports should provide current information through the last day of the previous month. Suggested report distribution is summarized in Table 7-1.

Management Report Use: Closing the Feedback Loop

Specific management actions are necessary to adjust project cost trends in order to assure that project costs remain under current control budget values. Since the general manager and department managers operate primarily at the primary and secondary account code levels, these reports must provide clear evidence of project status as well as clues to potential corrective remedies. The management summary reports provide the project status, while the predicted project overrun report provides the clues for corrective remedies.

Most of the data available in these reports are clearly identified by the column heading relative to a row description and account code. How-

Table 7-1
Cost Control Program Report Distribution

Report Title	Distribution
A. Individual Project Reports	
1. Project Data (Tertiary Accounts)	Respective Project Manager
2. Management Summary (Secondary Accounts)	Respective Project Manager Project Manager, Mgr. of Engineering, Sales Manager
3. Management Summary (Primary Accounts)	General Manager
4. Predicted Project Overruns	General Manager, Mgr. of Engineering, Sales Manager
5. Field Material	Construction Supervisor
B. Summary Reports (including all projects)	
1. Vendor Summary/ Expediting Report	Expeditor, Mgr. of Purchasing
2. Project Invoice Schedule	Accounting

(Left margin labels: Basic Cost Control Program; Cost Control Program By-Product Benefits; Cost Control Program)

ever, since many words have multiple interpretation, the reader should refer to the cost control glossary of terms presented in Chapter 2 for clarification. As a guideline, report use is summarized as follows:

A. Individual Project Reports
1. Project data (tertiary accounts)—cumulation of all project detail information for monthly line item updating.
2. Management summary (secondary accounts)—project cost and progress status summary for department-level managers.
3. Management summary (primary accounts)—project cost and progress status summary for top-level management (one-page report).
4. Predicted project overruns—specific listing by project of potential overrun line items. Used for determining cost correction strategy.
5. Field material report—listing of all project material. Used by field personnel to control project material.

B. Summary Reports (including all projects)
   1. Vendor summary/expediting report—groups all vendor entries for all projects. Used for expediting and determining if a vendor has received orders beyond his capacity.
   2. Project invoice schedule—summarizes invoice information for all projects by month and year. Assists in determining company cashflow forecast (one-page report).

Management should review closely three columns on the management summary reports—forecast over/under, committed amount, and budget portion. The forecast over/under column, which represents current control budget minus cost forecast, is a barometer of anticipated or predicted overruns or underruns. From this information, strategy can be planned to avoid overruns. At no time should management plan to absorb predicted overruns with predicted underruns. If this "make-up syndrome" is applied early in the project, it is likely that it will be repeated as the project progresses. Accounts scheduled to be committed during the later part of the project are forecast such that they absorb overruns of earlier commitments. Consequently, if these later accounts are not underrun, the result is unanticipated project overruns. Therefore, management should only concentrate on bringing overruns within the control budget value. The forecast over/under value is a prediction, not a fact. Management has time to make adjustments.

Data under committed amount and budget portion are history, and indicate the present cost position of the project. The budget portion value is that portion of the control budget that was allocated to those project expenditures already committed (as indicated by the committed amount value). Committed amount minus current budget portion (not shown on any report) yields the existing over- or underrun cost position of the project. A comparison of this historical value with the forecast over/under value will inform the manager of the following:

☐ Plans are in progress to correct an existing overrun.
☐ An existing overrun is expected to worsen.
☐ An existing underrun is expected to eventually overrun.
☐ The entire project is expected to underrun.
☐ It is possible for a poorly estimated project to break even with underruns absorbing overruns.

The predicted project overrun report is also provided to each corporate manager to specifically identify individual line items predicted to overrun. This information allows for two events to occur:

☐ Adjustments to be made immediately in current estimating for future projects to compensate.

☐ Management to provide specific suggestions to the project managers on steps to take in order to bring predicted (forecast) cost within the control budget value for each line item.

Management must react in a timely manner to the project cost control program in order to provide the control benefits intended. If management does not continuously respond, the program becomes a historical data reporting system, as the cost forecast value becomes the committed value instead of both becoming the budget value.

Project Postmortem

One of the most important pieces of documentation in any project is the project postmortem. This document is so named because it is filed when all signs indicate the project is finally "dead." However, projects are known to be extended after once being declared dead, thus requiring the modification and refiling of the postmortem after each "resurrection." It is a financial document developed after a project is complete that reflects project financial performance. In most instances, project personnel at the end of any project are psychologically ready to proceed to the next project, and have very little desire to complete a project postmortem. However, the postmortem, prepared by the project manager, is the one instrument that educates management as to the financial shortcomings of past projects, thereby contributing to improved estimating and predictions for future projects. In principle, this is application to the present what history has taught.

An example project postmortem report is illustrated in Figure 7-4. This is a representative project cost summary report for a completed project. The detailed cost data for a project postmortem would be attached to this summary when presented by the project manager to corporate management. A cursory review of data presented on the example project postmortem report should produce the following project financial conclusions:

☐ The project management (primary account code 1.0-0000) was probably originally accurately estimated. Increased project management cost was likely attributable to increased last-minute customer requirements since the overrun was not significant (from a percentage standpoint). However, on future projects of this type, the project management portion may need to be in the area of 6% rather than 5%.

☐ The engineering and design (primary account code 2.0-0000) effort was significantly overrun from an estimated value of 9% to actual value of 13.2%. This clearly indicates that the original estimate was low. However, future estimates should not be placed at 13 to 14% because historical data on a single project cannot be considered conclusive. The engineering and design estimate for the next project of this type should fall in the range of 11 to 12%.

COMPANY LOGO				Page _1_ of _1_

PROJECT COST SUMMARY

CUSTOMER _DEF Operating Company_   INSTALLATION SITE _Instl Oklahoma_

SALES PERSON _Joe Smith_   PROPOSAL NUMBER _BD-1142_

PROJECT COST BREAKDOWN	PROJECT CONTROL BUDGET Date: _11/15/82_ Currency: (_US $_)	% of Total Cost	PROJECT ACTUAL COST Date: _2/10/84_ Currency: (_US $_)	% of Total Cost
1.0-0000 Project Management	_1,685,000_	_5_	_2,346,000_	_6.4_
2.0-0000 Engineering and Design	_3,051,000_	_9_	_4,851,000_	_13.2_
3.0-0000 Purch. Equip. & Material	_9,153,000_	_27_	_8,244,000_	_22.4_
4.0-0000 Shop Fab. & Assembly	_5,085,000_	_15_	_5,143,000_	_14.0_
5.0-0000 Inspection & Testing	_338,000_	_1_	_285,000_	_<1_
6.0-0000 Packaging/Crating, Loading & Transportation	_—_	_—_	_102,000_	_<1_
7.0-0000 Field Construction	_687,000_	_2_	_478,000_	_1.3_
8.0-0000 Commercial	_13,560,000_	_40_	_13,031,000_	_35.4_
9.0-0000 Open (Customer Chg Order)	_338,000_	_1_	_330,000_	_<1_
	_—_	_—_	_2,043,000_	_5.5_
Cost Subtotal	_33,900,000_		_36,857,000_	
SALE PRICE SUBTOTAL (X _120_%)	_40,680,000_		_43,230,000_	
Passthrough Costs Contingency (% _5_ Cost Subtotal)	_1,685,000_		_1,695,000_	
	_—_		_—_	
	_—_		_—_	
	_—_		_—_	
Passthrough Subtotal	_0_	_—_	_0_	_—_
TOTAL SALE PRICE	_42,375,000_		_44,925,000_	
Project Schedule	_1/1/83 12/15/83_ Start to Finish (PLANNED)		_2/1/83 1/15/84_ Start to Finish (ACTUAL)	

PROJECT FINANCIAL ANALYSIS

Project Sale Price	_42,375,000_		_44,925,000_	
Budgeted Cost	_35,595,000_		_36,857,000_	
Gross Margin	_6,780,000_	_16_ %	_8,068,000_	_18.0_ %
Overhead Cost	_2,312,000_	_5.5_ %	_3,528,000_	_7.9_ %
Net Profit Before Taxes	_4,468,000_	_10.5_ %	_4,540,000_	_10.1_ %
Currency Exchange Rate & Date	_—_ _/_		_—_ _/_	

REFERENCE DATA: APPROVED FOR SALE:

Customer Inquiry No: _E21-67_ Date: _8/12/82_   By: _____ Date: _11/16/82_

Prepared By: _John Doe_   By: _____ Date: _11/17/82_

Figure 7-4. Example project postmortem report.

☐ The purchasing and fabricating accounts as well as other service accounts and field construction (primary account codes 3.0-0000 through 7.0-0000) all were completed for less than budgeted cost. This is good; however, a significant reduction (i.e., 27 to 22.4%) is evident in the purchased equipment and material area. If the project did not transcend economic entry into a recessionary period, this would indicate very conservative estimating in this area. This estimating area may also need attention in estimating new projects, since ultra-conservative estimating hampers competitive pricing of a project.

☐ The open account allocated to customer change orders (primary account code 9.0-0000) indicates that the estimated project scope of work was fairly accurate, since only 5.5% customer change orders were necessary.

☐ A review of the sale price differential (control budget sale price minus actual cost sale price) relative to the customer change order cost indicates that customer change order margins were maintained above 20%. This represents good project management since the original margin was maintained.

☐ Under project financial analysis it is apparent that the gross margin was improved through making the contingency available for application to the margin (i.e., project cost underruns absorbed overruns without the use of the contingency). The overhead cost was significantly increased (i.e., 5.5% to 7.9%). If this increase was not due to an unusual or one-time corporate financial distribution, future estimated project overhead costs may need increasing. An acceptable net profit margin (10%) was maintained for the project.

☐ Overall project financial performance was good.

A project postmortem of this type can be performed for any project. The information available to management to improve future project estimating, which translates into sales volume and profit, is significant.

To ignore this final project step is to ignore the lessons of history and to remain at the same level of proficiency rather than to improve.

Appendix A
Example of General Chart of Accounts

Index

Note: Detail account codes (0.0-00XX) not listed; used for defining line items or tasks for each project.

Section A-1
Primary Account Codes

Primary Account Code	Description
1.0-0000	Project Management
2.0-0000	Engineering and Design
3.0-0000	Purchased Equipment and Material
4.0-0000	Shop Fabrication and Assembly
5.0-0000	Inspection and Testing
6.0-0000	Packaging/Crating, Loading and Transportation

7.0-0000	Field Construction
8.0-0000	Commercial
9.0-0000	Open

Section A-2
Secondary Account Codes

Secondary Account Code	Description
1.0-0000	Project Management
1.1-0000	Management
1.2-0000	Purchasing and Expediting
1.3-0000	Cost and Schedule Control
1.4-0000	Fabrication or Construction Coordination
1.5-0000	Open
1.6-0000	Open
1.7-0000	Open
1.8-0000	Open
1.9-0000	Expenses
2.0-0000	Engineering and Design
2.1-0000	Payroll Personnel
2.2-0000	Indirect Personnel
2.3-0000	Consultants
2.4-0000	Open
2.5-0000	Open
2.6-0000	Open
2.7-0000	Open
2.8-0000	Open
2.9-0000	Expenses
3.0-0000	Purchased Equipment and Material
3.1-0000	Major Equipment
3.2-0000	Minor Equipment
3.3-0000	Commodity Materials
3.4-0000	Open
3.5-0000	Open
3.6-0000	Open
3.7-0000	Open
3.8-0000	Open
3.9-0000	Open

4.0-0000	Shop Fabrication and Assembly
4.1-0000	Buildings
4.2-0000	Structural
4.3-0000	Equipment Placement and Component Assembly
4.4-0000	Piping
4.5-0000	Instrumentation
4.6-0000	Electrical
4.7-0000	Open
4.8-0000	Open
4.9-0000	Open
5.0-0000	Inspection and Testing
5.1-0000	Inspection
5.2-0000	Testing
5.3-0000	Open
5.4-0000	Open
5.5-0000	Open
5.6-0000	Open
5.7-0000	Open
5.8-0000	Open
5.9-0000	Open
6.0-0000	Packaging/Crating, Loading, and Transportation
6.1-0000	Packaging/Crating
6.2-0000	Loading
6.3-0000	Transportation
6.4-0000	Open
6.5-0000	Open
6.6-0000	Open
6.7-0000	Open
6.8-0000	Open
6.9-0000	Open
7.0-0000	Field Construction
7.1-0000	Indirect Costs and Temporary Construction
7.2-0000	Site Preparation, Concrete, and Earthwork
7.3-0000	Building Installation
7.4-0000	Structural Steel Installation
7.5-0000	Equipment Placement
7.6-0000	Piping Installation
7.7-0000	Instruments and Controls Installation
7.8-0000	Electrical Installation

7.9-0000	Insulation, Fireproofing, Refractory Installation, and Painting
8.0-0000	Commercial
8.1-0000	Bonds
8.2-0000	Taxes
8.3-0000	Customs Duties
8.4-0000	Agent Fees
8.5-0000	Insurance
8.6-0000	Translation
8.7-0000	Warranty
8.8-0000	Open
8.9-0000	Open
9.0-0000	Open

Section A-3
Tertiary Account Codes

Tertiary Account Code	Description
1.0-0000	Project Management
1.1-0000	Management
1.1-1000	Project Manager
1.1-2000	Project Secretary
1.1-3000 through 1.1-9000	Open Accounts
1.2-0000	Purchasing and Expediting
1.2-1000	Purchasing
1.2-2000	Expediting
1.2-3000	Quality Control
1.2-4000	Secretarial
1.2-5000	Clerical
1.2-6000 through 1.2-9000	Open Accounts

1.3-0000	Cost and Schedule Control
1.3-1000	Project Accounting
1.3-2000	Cost Engineering and Reporting
1.3-3000	Scheduling and Reporting
1.3-4000 through 1.3-9000	Open Accounts

1.4-0000	Fabrication or Construction Coordination
1.4-1000	Construction Supervisor
1.4-2000	Construction Engineer
1.4-3000	Construction Coordinator
1.4-4000	Secretarial
1.4-5000	Clerical
1.4-6000 through 1.4-9000	Open Accounts
1.5-0000 through 1.8-0000	Open Accounts

1.9-0000	Expenses
1.9-1000	Travel and Living Expenses
1.9-1100	Project Manager
1.9-1200	Purchasing and Expediting
1.9-1300	Scheduling and Cost Control
1.9-1400	Fabrication or Construction Coordination
1.9-1500 through 1.9-1900	Open Accounts
1.9-2000	Relocation Expenses
1.9-3000	Reproduction and Reproduction Materials (Printing, Blueprints, Reductions, etc.)
1.9-4000	Computer Usage
1.9-4100	Expediting
1.9-4200	Cost Control
1.9-4300	Scheduling
1.9-4400 through 1.9-4900	Open Accounts
1.9-5000	Communications (Telephone, Telex, Mail, Courier, etc.)

1.9-6000 through 1.9-9000	Open Accounts
2.0-0000	Engineering and Design
2.1-0000	Payroll Personnel
2.1-1000	Engineering
2.1-1100	Project Engineer
2.1-1200	Process Engineer
2.1-1300	Mechanical Engineer
2.1-1400	Instrument Engineer
2.1-1500	Electrical Engineer
2.1-1600	Structural Engineer
2.1-1700	Civil Engineer
2.1-1800	Startup Engineer
2.1-1900	Technical Writing for Manuals and Studies
2.1-2000	Design and Drafting
2.1-2100	Project Planning, Cost, and Scheduling
2.1-2200	Flow Sheets
2.1-2300	Layouts, Plot Plans
2.1-2400	Piping
2.1-2500	Instrumentation
2.1-2600	Electrical
2.1-2700	Structural
2.1-2800	Civil
2.1-2900	Manuals
2.1-3000 through 2.1-9000	Open Accounts
2.2-0000	Indirect Personnel
2.2-1000	Engineering
2.2-1100	Project Engineer
2.2-1200	Process Engineer
2.2-1300	Mechanical Engineer
2.2-1400	Instrument Engineer
2.2-1500	Electrical Engineer
2.2-1600	Structural Engineer
2.2-1700	Civil Engineer
2.2-1800	Startup Engineer
2.2-1900	Technical Writing for Manuals and Studies
2.2-2000	Design and Drafting

2.2-2100	Project Planning, Cost, and Scheduling
2.2-2200	Flow Sheets
2.2-2300	Layouts, Plot Plans
2.2-2400	Piping
2.2-2500	Instrumentation
2.2-2600	Electrical
2.2-2700	Structural
2.2-2800	Civil
2.2-2900	Manuals
2.2-3000	
through	
2.2-9000	Open Accounts
2.3-0000	Consultants
2.3-1000	Engineering
2.3-1100	Project Engineer
2.3-1200	Process Engineer
2.3-1300	Mechanical Engineer
2.3-1400	Instrument Engineer
2.3-1500	Electrical Engineer
2.3-1600	Structural Engineer
2.3-1700	Civil Engineer
2.3-1800	Startup Engineer
2.3-1900	Technical Writing for Manuals and Studies
2.3-2000	Design and Drafting
2.3-2100	Project Planning, Cost, and Scheduling
2.3-2200	Flow Sheets
2.3-2300	Layouts, Plot Plans
2.3-2400	Piping
2.3-2500	Instrumentation
2.3-2600	Electrical
2.3-2700	Structural
2.3-2800	Civil
2.3-2900	Manuals
2.3-3000	
through	
2.8-0000	Open Accounts
2.9-0000	Expenses
2.9-1000	Travel and Living Expenses
2.9-1100	Project Engineer
2.9-1200	Design Engineer (Process, Mechanical, etc.)
2.9-1300	Designer

2.9-1400	Consultant
2.9-1500	Reproduction and Reproduction Materials (Xerox, Printing, Blueprints, Reductions, etc.)
2.9-1600	Manual Covers, Dividers, etc. (Includes translation costs)
2.9-1700	Computer Usage
2.9-1800	Communications (Telephone, Telex, Mail, Courier, etc.)
2.9-1900	Open Accounts
3.0-0000	Purchased Equipment and Material
3.1-0000	Major Equipment
3.1-1000	Tanks (Atmospheric)
3.1-1100	Vertical Tanks
3.1-1200	Horizontal Tanks
3.1-1300 through 3.1-1900	Open Accounts
3.1-2000	Pressure Vessels
3.1-2100	Scrubbers
3.1-2200	Pulsation
3.1-2300	Filter Bottles
3.1-2400	Towers
3.1-2500	Separators
3.1-2600	Pressure Storage Tanks
3.1-2700	Vessel Internals
3.1-2800 through 3.1-2900	Open Accounts
3.1-3000	Heat Transfer Equipment
3.1-3100	Fired Heaters
3.1-3200	Boilers
3.1-3300	Heat Exchangers
3.1-3400	Air Coolers
3.1-3500	Cooling Towers
3.1-3600 through 3.1-3900	Open Accounts
3.1-4000	Rotating and Mechanical Equipment
3.1-4100	Pumps (Centrifugal, Positive Displacement, etc.)
3.1-4200	Electric Motors
3.1-4300	Generators
3.1-4400	Generator Drives

3.1-4500	Generator Sets
3.1-4600	Gear Boxes
3.1-4700	Starting Air/Gas Motors
3.1-4800	Air Compressors and Drives
3.1-4900	Open Account
3.1-5000	Miscellaneous Mechanical Equipment
3.1-5100	Cranes
3.1-5200	Filters
3.1-5300	Silencers
3.1-5400	Strainers
3.1-5500 through 3.1-5900	Open Accounts
3.1-6000	Packaged Systems
3.1-6100	Lube and Seal Oil System, Console Assembly (Including Fabrication)
3.1-6200	Dehydration System
3.1-6300	Chemical Injection System (Process and Firewater)
3.1-6400	Water Washing Gas Generator
3.1-6500	Sewage Treatment System
3.1-6600	Water Treating System
3.1-6700	Pollution Control
3.1-6800	Fire Detection/Prevention System
3.1-6900	Gas Detection System
3.1-7000	Prefabricated Buildings (Control Room, MCC, Office or Quarters Building)
3.1-7100	Structural
3.1-7200	Plumbing
3.1-7300	Electrical
3.1-7400	Fixtures
3.1-7500	Ventilation Fans and Louvers
3.1-7600	Heating and Air Conditioning
3.1-7700 through 3.1-7900	Open Accounts
3.1-8000 through 3.1-9000	Open Accounts
3.2-0000	Minor Equipment
3.2-1000	Valves and Piping Specialties
3.2-1100	Automatic Valves (With Actuators)
3.2-1200	Manual Valves

3.2-1300	Specialty Valves
3.2-1400	Piping Specialties
3.2-1500	
through	
3.2-1900	Open Accounts
3.2-2000	Instruments and Controls
3.2-2100	Pressure Instruments
3.2-2200	Temperature Instruments
3.2-2300	Flow Instruments
3.2-2400	Level Instruments
3.2-2500	Control Panels
3.2-2600	Miscellaneous
3.2-2700	
through	
3.2-2900	Open Accounts
3.2-3000	Electrical Equipment
3.2-3100	Motor Control Center (MCC)
3.2-3200	Uninterruptible Power Supply (UPS)
3.2-3300	Switchgear
3.2-3400	Batteries
3.2-3500	Battery Chargers
3.2-3600	Distribution Panels
3.2-3700	Junction Boxes
3.2-3800	Lights
3.2-3900	Power Transformers
3.2-4000	Miscellaneous
3.2-5000	
through	
3.2-9000	Open
3.3-0000	Commodity Materials
3.3-1000	Foundation Materials
3.3-2000	Structural Materials
3.3-3000	Pipe, Flanges and Fittings
3.3-3100	Pipe (Non-Structural)
3.3-3200	Flanges
3.3-3300	Fittings
3.3-3400	Studs and Nuts
3.3-3500	Gaskets
3.3-3600	
through	
3.3-3900	Open Accounts
3.3-4000	Protective Coatings

3.3-4100	Paint
3.3-4200	Galvanize
3.3-4300	Insulation
3.3-4400	
through	
3.3-4900	Open Accounts
3.3-5000	Instrument Installation Materials
3.3-5100	Instrument Tubing and Fittings
3.3-5200	Conduit and Fittings
3.3-5300	Wire
3.3-5400	Cable Trays
3.3-5500	
through	
3.3-5900	Open Accounts
3.3-6000	Electrical Installation Material
3.3-6100	Conduit and Fittings
3.3-6200	Wiring
3.3-6300	Bus Duct
3.3-6400	Cable Trays
3.3-6500	
through	
3.3-6900	Open Accounts
3.3-7000	Nameplates
3.3-8000	Lubricants, Fuels and Chemicals
3.3-8100	Lubricants
3.3-8200	Fuels
3.3-8300	Chemicals
3.3-8400	Catalysts
3.3-8500	
through	
3.3-8900	Open Accounts
3.3-9000	Open Account
4.0-0000	Shop Fabrication and Packaging
4.1-0000	Buildings
4.2-0000	Structural
4.3-0000	Equipment Placement and Component Assembly
4.4-0000	Piping
4.5-0000	Instrumentation

4.6-0000	Electrical
5.0-0000	Inspection and Testing
5.1-0000	Inspection
5.1-1000	Mechanical
5.1-2000	X-Ray
5.1-3000	Ultrasonic
5.2-0000	Testing
5.2-1000	Run Test
5.2-2000	Performance Test
5.2-3000	Testing Materials
5.2-4000 through 5.2-9000	Open Accounts
6.0-0000	Packaging/Crating, Loading and Transportation
6.1-0000	Export Crating
6.2-0000	Loading
6.3-0000	Transportation
7.0-0000	Field Construction
7.1-0000	Indirect Costs & Temporary Construction
7.1-1000	Field Office Expense
7.1-1100	Office Furniture Rental
7.1-1200	Water Cooler Rental
7.1-1300	Office Supplies
7.1-1400	Communications Expenses (Telephone, Telex, Mail, Courier, etc.)
7.1-1500	Reproduction (Printing, Blueprints, Reductions, etc.)
7.1-1600	Other
7.1-1700 through 7.1-1900	Open Accounts
7.1-2000	First Aid Expense
7.1-3000	Expendable Construction Supplies and Equipment (Small Tools and Consummables)

7.1-4000	Surplus Material Expense
7.1-5000	General Expense
7.1-6000	Mobilization/Demobilization (Hauling, Personnel Transfer Cost, Surplus Material Handling, etc.)
7.1-7000	Plant Access
7.1-7100	Temporary Roads (For Construction)
7.1-7200	Railroad Sidings (For Construction)
7.1-7300 through	
7.1-7900	Open Accounts
7.1-8000	Miscellaneous Facilities
7.1-8100	Fencing (For Construction Site)
7.1-8200	Water Wells (For Construction Site)
7.1-8300	Septic Tanks (For Construction Site)
7.1-8400 through	
7.1-8900	Open Accounts
7.1-9000	Temporary Facilities (For Construction Site)
7.1-9100	Temporary Buildings—Field Trailer
7.1-9200	Temporary Sanitary Facilities
7.1-9300	Temporary Docks and Platforms
7.1-9400	Temporary Utilities
7.1-9500	Other Temporary Facilities
7.1-9600 through	
7.1-9900	Open Accounts
7.2-0000	Site Preparation, Concrete, and Earthwork
7.2-1000	Plant Site Preparation
7.2-1100	Clearing
7.2-1200	Rough Leveling and Finish Grading
7.2-1300	Drainage
7.2-1400	Miscellaneous
7.2-1500	Area Surfacing
7.2-1600	Plant Access (Permanent Roads, Parking Areas, and Railroad Sidings)
7.2-1700	Fencing (Plant Enclosure)
7.2-1800	Water Wells (For Plant Operation)
7.2-1900	Septic Tanks (For Plant Operation)
7.2-2000	Area Clean Up
7.2-2100	Daily Clean Up (Construction Area)
7.2-2200	Final Clean Up (Construction Area)
7.2-2300	

through	
7.2-2900	Open Accounts
7.2-3000	Excavation and Backfill
7.2-3100	Machine Excavation and Backfill
7.2-3200	Hand Excavation and Backfill
7.2-3300	Sheet Piling, Shoring, Pumping Out, etc.
7.2-3400	Fill (Imported)
7.2-3500	
through	
7.2-3900	Open Accounts
7.2-4000	Sub-Foundation Structures
7.2-4100	Bearing Piles
7.2-4200	Caissons
7.2-4300	
through	
7.2-4900	Open Accounts
7.2-5000	Forming and Stripping
7.2-6000	Reinforcing Steel Placement
7.2-6100	Reinforcing Rod, etc.
7.2-6200	Wire Mesh
7.2-6300	
through	
7.2-6900	Open Accounts
7.2-7000	Anchor Bolts, Inserts and Miscellaneous
7.2-7100	Anchor Bolts
7.2-7200	Other Structural and Pipe Inserts
7.2-7300	Elastite
7.2-7400	Waterproofing Membrane
7.2-7500	Water Stop
7.2-7600	
through	
7.2-7900	Open Accounts
7.2-8000	Concrete
7.2-8100	Mass Concrete—Major Foundations
7.2-8200	Walls and Columns
7.2-8300	Floors, Sidewalks, and Slabs on Grade
7.2-8400	Elevated Floors and Structures
7.2-8500	Small Foundations (less than 1 cu. yd.)
7.2-8600	Conduit Encasements
7.2-8700	Trenches and Sumps
7.2-8800	Special Finishing Procedures
7.2-8900	Testing
7.2-9000	Grouting

7.2-9100	Rotating Equipment
7.2-9200	Vessels and Other Equipment
7.2-9300	Structures and Structural Supports
7.2-9400	
through	
7.2-9900	Open Accounts

7.3-0000   Building Installation

7.3-1000	Structural Steel Buildings
7.3-2000	Masonry Buildings
7.3-3000	Frame Buildings
7.3-4000	Building Furnishings
7.3-5000	Shelters
7.3-6000	
through	
7.3-9000	Open Accounts

7.4-0000   Structural Steel Installation

7.4-1000	Towers
7.4-2000	Platforms
7.4-3000	Major Structures
7.4-4000	Equipment Supports
7.4-5000	Ladders, Handrails and Stairways
7.4-6000	Floor Plate and Grating
7.4-6100	Floor Plate
7.4-6200	Grating (Not on Skids or Prefabbed Platforms)
7.4-6300	Trench and Sump Covers
7.4-6400	
through	
7.4-6900	Open Accounts
7.4-7000	Pipe Supports and Stanchions
7.4-7100	Pipe Racks
7.4-7200	Individual Pipe Stanchions
7.4-7300	
through	
7.4-7900	Open Accounts
7.4-8000	
through	
7.4-9000	Open Accounts

7.5-0000   Equipment Placement

7.5-1000	Equipment Placement
7.5-1100	Tanks

7.5-1200	Vessels
7.5-1300	Heat Transfer Equipment
7.5-1400	Rotating Equipment
7.5-1500	Packaged Systems
7.5-1600	Crane Rental
7.5-1700	Truck Rental and Demurrage
7.5-1800	
through	
7.5-1900	Open Accounts
7.5-2000	
through	
7.5-9000	Open Accounts

7.6-0000	Pipe Installation
7.6-1000	Above Ground Pipe Installation and Welding
7.6-1100	Valve Placement, etc.
7.6-1200	
through	
7.6-1900	Open Accounts
7.6-2000	Other Operations
7.6-2100	Unloading, Hauling, and Warehousing
7.6-2200	Machine Excavation and Backfill
7.6-2300	Hand Excavation and Backfill
7.6-2400	Supports and Hangers (including materials)
7.6-2500	Underground Coating
7.6-2600	Testing of Welds and Piping
7.6-2700	Steam Tracing
7.6-2800	Stress Relieving
7.6-2900	Radiographing
7.6-3000	Scaffolding
7.6-4000	Underground Piping Installation
7.6-4100	Carbon Steel and Alloy U.G.
7.6-4200	Concrete Pipe
7.6-4300	Fire Hydrants and Accessories
7.6-4400	Other Underground Accessories
7.6-4500	
through	
7.6-4900	Open Accounts
7.6-5000	
through	
7.6-9000	Open Accounts

7.7-0000	Instruments and Controls Installation
7.7-1000	Instrument Installation
7.7-1100	Pneumatic
7.7-1200	Electronic
7.7-1300 through 7.7-1900	Open Accounts
7.7-2000	Control Panel Installation
7.7-2100	Pneumatic
7.7-2200	Electronic
7.7-2300 through 7.7-2900	Open Accounts
7.7-3000	Weather Protection for Field Mounted Instruments
7.7-4000	Testing and Calibration
7.7-5000 through 7.7-9000	Open Accounts
7.8-0000	Electrical Installation
7.8-1000	Grounding Only
7.8-1100	Excavation and Backfill
7.8-1200	Grounding Wire Installation & Connection
7.8-1300 through 7.8-1900	Open Accounts
7.8-2000	Power Equipment Installation
7.8-2100	Transformers
7.8-2200	Motor Control Center
7.8-2300	High Voltage Switchgear (Above 600V)
7.8-2400	Bus Bars, Metal Clad Switch Gear, Main Switching Devices, Starters, Interrupting Devices, Capacitors, Arrestors, Relays, etc.
7.8-2500	Low-Voltage Switchgear (700V and Below)
7.8-2600	Switches, Circuit Breakers, Starters, Relays, Panel Boards, etc.
7.8-2700 through 7.8-2900	Open Accounts
7.8-3000 through 7.8-4000	Open Accounts
7.8-5000	Power Distribution Installation

7.8-5100	Conduit and Fittings
7.8-5200	Cable and Fittings
7.8-5300	Pull Boxes
7.8-5400	Control Stations
7.8-5500	Power Pole Installation
7.8-5600	Miscellaneous Hardware
7.8-5700	Panelboards, Junction Boxes, Outlet and Switch Boxes, Terminations, Splices, Clamps, etc.
7.8-5800 through 7.8-5900	Open Accounts
7.8-6000	Lighting Installation
7.8-6100	Conduit and Fittings
7.8-6200	Cable and Fittings
7.8-6300	Pull Boxes
7.8-6400	Fixtures, Receptacles, Switches and Panel Boards
7.8-6500	Poles and Fixtures for Area Lighting
7.8-6600	Miscellaneous Lighting Requirements
7.8-6700 through 7.8-6900	Open Accounts
7.8-7000	Communications Installation
7.8-7100	Conduit and Fittings
7.8-7200	Cable and Fittings
7.8-7300	Pull Boxes
7.8-7400	Telephone Equipment
7.8-7500	Radio Equipment
7.8-7600	Public Address Equipment
7.8-7700	Fire Warning System
7.8-7800	Miscellaneous
7.8-7900	Open Account
7.8-8000	Electrical Supports and Racks Installation
7.8-8100	Supports, Brackets and Racks for Switchgear and Transformers
7.8-8200	Conduit Supports and Racks (including Cable Trays)
7.8-8300	Miscellaneous
7.8-8400 through 7.8-8900	Open Accounts
7.8-9000	Open Account

<u>7.9-0000</u>	<u>Insulation, Fireproofing, Refractory Installation, and</u>
	<u>Painting</u>
7.9-1000	Piping Insulation
7.9-1100	Hot Pipe
7.9-1200	Cold Pipe
7.9-1300	Personnel Protection Only
7.9-1400	.
through	
7.9-1900	Open Accounts
7.9-2000	Vessel Insulation
7.9-2100	Hot Vessels, Exchangers and Heaters
7.9-2200	Cold Vessels and Exchangers
7.9-2300	Personnel Protection Only
7.9-2400	
through	
7.9-2900	Open Accounts
7.9-3000	Fireproofing
7.9-3100	Formed Concrete
7.9-3200	Gunite
7.9-3300	Plastering (Hand)
7.9-3400	Other (Specify)
7.9-3500	
through	
7.9-3900	Open Accounts
7.9-4000	Refractory
7.9-4100	Refractory Lining of Pipe
7.9-4200	Refractory Lining of Equipment (unless supplied with equipment)
7.9-4300	
through	
7.9-4900	Open Accounts
7.9-5000	Painting
7.9-5100	Structures
7.9-5200	Vessels, Exchangers, Furnaces and Boilers
7.9-5300	Mechanical Equipment
7.9-5400	Piping
7.9-5500	Buildings
7.9-5600	Others (Specify)
7.9-5700	
through	
7.9-5900	Open Accounts

7.9-6000 through 7.9-9000	Open Accounts
8.0-0000	Commercial
8.1-0000	Bonds
8.2-0000	Taxes
8.3-0000	Customs Duties
8.4-0000	Agent Fees
8.5-0000	Insurance
8.6-0000	Translation
8.7-0000	Warranty
8.8-0000 through 8.9-0000	Open Accounts
9.0-0000	Open Account

Appendix B
Project Cost Control Forms

Sales

1. Project Cost Summary
2. Project Detail Estimate—Project Management & Engineering/Design
3. Project Detail Estimate—Personnel Expenses
4. Project Detail Estimate—Purchased Equipment & Material and Subcontracts
5. Project Management (PM) Instruction Transmittal

Project Management

1. Material Requisition (MR)
2. Fabrication or Field Construction Subcontract Required Pricing Breakdown (Inquiry Insert)
3. Preferred Subcontractor/Vendor Transmittal
4. Purchase Order
5. Customer Change Request/Order
6. Drawing List & Status Report
7. Equipment Status Report
8. Project Overrun Request
9. Time Summary (Used by all Applied Personnel)
10. Minutes of Meeting
11. Cost Control Program—Monthly Cost and Progress Reports
    • Management Summary Report—Primary Accounts
    • Management Summary Report—Secondary Accounts
    • Management Summary Report—Tertiary Accounts
    • Predicted Project Overrun Report
    • Field Material Report
    • Vendor Summary/Expediting Report
    • Project Invoice Schedule

Form B-1 Use and Data Entry Guidelines

Purpose and Use

This form is used for two purposes—to establish the initial project cost and sale price and to compare that initial cost data with the actual cost data after the project is complete. The data presented on this form are supported by detail data presented on Forms B-2, B-3, and B-4.

Data Entry

The form entries are self-explanatory by the column and row titles:

Customer-related information is entered at the top of the form and reference data in the bottom left corner.

The summarized project control budget is entered, in accordance with the chart of accounts in the appropriate column. The budget number, date, and currency should be entered at the top of the column used. Once all project cost data are entered, the % of total cost is calculated by first adding those cost entries opposite the % entries to obtain a total cost. Next, calculate the % of the total for each cost entry.

Row entries are self-explanatory as titled. Extra lines are available under passthrough costs for unexpected entries. The sale price subtotal is calculated by multiplying the cost subtotal by the established markup. All row % blanks should be filled in after cost values are entered in the column.

Reference information data should be completed in the lower left corner.

The project control budget must be approved for sale.

```
  ╭─────────╮                    B-1
 ( COMPANY )
  ╲  LOGO  ╱                                 Page ___ of ___
   ╲──────╱
                    PROJECT COST SUMMARY
CUSTOMER_____    INSTALLATION SITE_____

SALES PERSON_____    PROPOSAL NUMBER_____
```

PROJECT COST BREAKDOWN	PROJECT CONTROL BUDGET		PROJECT ACTUAL COST	
	Date:_____	% of	Date:_____	% of
	Currency:	Total	Currency:	Total
	(_____)	Cost	(_____)	Cost
1.0-0000 Project Management				
2.0-0000 Engineering and Design				
3.0-0000 Purch. Equip. & Material				
4.0-0000 Shop Fab. & Assembly				
5.0-0000 Inspection & Testing				
6.0-0000 Packaging/Crating, Loading & Transportation				
7.0-0000 Field Construction				
8.0-0000 Commercial				
9.0-0000 Open				
Cost Subtotal				
SALE PRICE SUBTOTAL (X ___%)				
Passthrough Costs Contingency (%___Cost Subtotal)				
Passthrough Subtotal				
TOTAL SALE PRICE				
Project Schedule	/ / to / /		/ / to / /	
	Start to Finish (PLANNED)		Start to Finish (ACTUAL)	

```
PROJECT FINANCIAL ANALYSIS ─────────────────────────────────

Project Sale Price       _____        _____
Budgeted Cost            _____        _____
Gross Margin             _____  %     _____  %
Overhead Cost            _____  %     _____  %
Net Profit Before Taxes  _____  %     _____  %
Currency Exchange Rate & Date  _____ / /    _____ / /
```

REFERENCE DATA:	APPROVED FOR SALE:
Customer Inquiry No:_____ Date: / /	By:_____ Date: / /
Prepared By:_____	By:_____ Date: / /

Form B-2 Use and Data Entry Guidelines

Purpose and Use

This form is used for estimating labor only. This labor may be associated with project management (e.g., project management, purchasing, cost and schedule control, and field coordination), or engineering/design.

Data Entry

Each project estimate line item detail is entered on a row. Line item groupings may also be established, if not previously established by the chart of accounts. Each row description must be accompanied by an account code (according to the chart of accounts) and manhours with charge rate and estimated cost data. If data need to be displayed in a foreign currency, enter a foreign currency designator beside the estimated cost for each row. Note the definition of the foreign currency designator at the bottom of the page. Values may be subtotaled at the bottom of each page, as convenient.

B-2

PROJECT DETAIL ESTIMATE

Customer:_____

Proposal No:_____

Page ___ of ___

COMPANY
LOGO

PROJECT MANAGEMENT
AND ENGINEERING/DESIGN
(LABOR ONLY)

ACCOUNT CODE

Primary	Secondary	Tertiary	Detail	CATEGORY OR ITEM DESCRIPTION	Req'd. Manpower (MH)	Charge Rate ($/HR)	Estimated Cost ($)

Form B-3 Use and Data Entry Guidelines

Purpose and Use

This form is used for estimating personnel expenses (i.e., account codes 1.9 and 2.9) only. There are several categories of expenses, as indicated under codes 1.9 and 2.9 in the chart of accounts.

Data Entry

Each project estimate line item detail is entered on a row. Line item groupings may also be established, if not previously established by the chart of accounts. Each row description must be accompanied by an account code (according to the chart of accounts) and quantity with rate and estimated cost. Each quantity and rate value must have unit definition (e.g., number of trips, number of days of travel, cost/trip, cost/day, and number of computer runs) for each row. Each estimated expense must have a currency definition for each row. Values may be subtotaled at the bottom of each page, as convenient.

B-3

Customer:_____

Proposal No:_____

Page ___ of ___

PROJECT DETAIL ESTIMATE

PERSONNEL EXPENSES

ACCOUNT CODE

Primary	Secondary	Tertiary	Detail	CATEGORY OR ITEM DESCRIPTION	Quantity (With Units)	Rate (With Units)	Estimated Cost (Specify Currency)

COMPANY LOGO

Form B-4 Use and Data Entry Guidelines

Purpose and Use

This form is used for purchased equipment, material, and subcontracts only. The categories for these are listed under primary codes 3.0 through 9.0 in the chart of accounts.

Data Entry

Each project estimate line item detail is entered on a row. Line item groupings may also be established, if not previously established, by the chart of accounts. Each row description must be accompanied by an account code (according to the chart of accounts), a cost data source identification, date the cost data source was received, quantity, and estimated cost. The cost data source may be verbal from a phone conversation, a written quotation, in-house historical files, or from other sources. As much information as possible should be given in this column to identify the source. The quantity value is the number of units described in the description column. The currency should be specified by row in the estimated cost column.

If a detailed manpower and material estimate is needed in lieu of subcontract costs, supporting estimate forms should be attached to this form (which is then considered a summary).

B-4   Customer:_____

Proposal No:_____

(COMPANY LOGO)

Page ___ of ___

PROJECT DETAIL ESTIMATE

PURCHASED EQUIPMENT,
MATERIAL AND SUBCONTRACTS

ACCOUNT CODE

Primary	Secondary	Tertiary	Detail	CATEGORY OR ITEM DESCRIPTION	Cost Data Source	Date Source Rec'd.	Qty.	Estimated Cost (Specify Currency)

Form B-5 Use and Data Entry Guidelines

Purpose and Use

This form is used for formally transmitting the project management instructions from the sales department to the engineering department. The form must be signed by the manager of each department for the transmittal to be complete.

Data Entry

Pertinent project data are entered at the top of the form (self-explanatory).

Each document name to be transmitted must be listed on a row accompanied by an identifying number, number of pages, original issue date, and any pertinent comments. Specific documents that must be a part of the transmittal are listed on the form; other document names may be written in.

The manager of sales and manager of engineering signatures with date, as well as the name of the assigned project manager or project engineer, must be placed at the bottom of the form for the transmittal to be complete.

Each department shall keep a copy of the completed transmittal form and all transmitted documents. A copy of the completed transmittal form shall be sent to the general manager for his files.

B-5

(COMPANY LOGO)

PROJECT MANAGEMENT INSTRUCTIONS TRANSMITTAL

CUSTOMER:_____   INSTALLATION SITE:_____

SALES PERSON:_____   PROPOSAL NO:_____

ESTIMATOR:_____   INITIAL CONTROL BUDGET TOTAL:_____

INFORMATION TRANSMITTED:

Identifying Number	Document Name	No. of Pages	Original Issue Date	Comments
	Quotation (Final Updated Copy)			
	Customer Inquiry			
	Customer Specifications			
	Contract			
	Initial Control Budget			
	Vendor/Subcontractor Quotations			
	1)			
	2)			
	3)			
	4)			
	5)			
	Other			
	1)			
	2)			
	3)			
	4)			
	5)			

SALES DEPAREMENT:
TRANSMITTED -

By:_____

Date:_____

Copy to: General Manager

ENGINEERING DEPARTMENT:
REVIEWED AND ACCEPTED -

By:_____

Date:_____

Assigned Project Manager/Engineer

Form B-6 Use and Data Entry Guidelines

Purpose and Use

This form is used for requesting the purchase of equipment, materials, and subcontracts from the purchasing department. The form should be filled out in a manner that most clearly matches information displayed on the control budget; this will expedite approval.

Data Entry

Pertinent project information (self-explanatory) is entered at the top left of the form.

Material requisition information (i.e., number and status) is entered at the top center of the form.

Verification of the control budget values by sales is required at the top right of the form.

Each requested line item description is entered by row with associated account code (obtained from the control budget), quantity, and control budget value.

Subtotals may be placed at the bottom of each page, as is convenient.

B-6

MATERIAL REQUISITION (MR)

COMPANY LOGO

Date: _____
Page ____ of ____

CUSTOMER: _____
PROJECT NO. _____

REQUISITIONER

MATERIAL REQUISITION NUMBER

___ PRICE INQUIRY ONLY
___ PURCHASE REQUISITION
___ ORIGINAL ISSUE
___ ISSUE NO. _____

SALES COST CONTROL VERIFICATION

By: _____
Date: _____

Account Code	Quantity	Description	Comments	Control Budget

Form B-7 Use and Data Entry Guidelines

Purpose and Use

This form is used for formally transmitting the selection of a preferred subcontractor or vendor after quotations have been evaluated. Formal recording of this information is necessary for the project historical file.

Data Entry

Pertinent project information and to/from data (self-explanatory) is entered at the top of the form.

Each quotation evaluated is identified with quotation number, date, and price. An * is placed beside the row listing of the selected subcontractor or vendor.

A basis for the selection is offered. This explanation should be brief and highlight only the main reasons for the selection. A technical bid evaluation may be attached. Comments for clarification may be entered below.

Data describing the MR and control budget value for this item(s) is entered at the bottom of the form.

The preferred subcontractor/vendor price must be evaluated and verified by sales in the lower right corner.

B-7

```
(COMPANY LOGO)
```

PREFERRED
SUBCONTRACTOR/VENDOR
TRANSMITTAL

INTERNAL MEMO

Date:_____

Page ___ of ___

TO: PURCHASING DEPARTMENT

Attention _____

FROM:_____   Customer:_____
Evaluator

_____   Project No._____
Department

THE FOLLOWING QUOTATIONS HAVE BEEN EVALUATED:

Quotation Number	Vendor Name	Quotation Date	Total Quoted Price	Preferred Vendor (*)

BASIS FOR VENDOR SELECTION:

COMMENTS:

MATERIAL REQUISITION: **PRICE OF PREFERRED VENDOR IS:**
Number:_____
                                     OVER (amount)_____
Date: _____   UNDER(amount)_____

Note: Technical Bid Tabulation   **CONTROL BUDGET VALUE**
       Attached (if applicable)   **VERIFIED BY SALES**_____

B-8

PURCHASE ORDER

COMPANY LOGO

EXAMPLE FORMAT ONLY

TO:

PURCHASE ORDER NO. _____

PAGE ___ OF ___

DATE OF ORDER ___/___/___

REQUIRED AT DESTINATION ___/___/___

F.O.B. _____

SHIP TO:

SHIP VIA _____

BILLING ADDRESS:

_____

_____

_____

ACCOUNT CODE	QUANTITY	DESCRIPTION	UNIT PRICE	TOTAL

THIS ORDER IS SUBJECT TO ALL TERMS AND CONDITIONS ON THE REVERSE SIDE HEREOF.

IF FURTHER INFORMATION IS REQUIRED, CONTACT:

AUTHORIZATION:

_____
GENERAL MANAGER (as applicable)

_____
PURCHASING MANAGER

B-9

CUSTOMER CHANGE ORDER

CHANGE ORDER NO.
Page ___ of ___

Customer:_____   Project No._____
                                      Customer
Installation Site:_____   Contract No._____

Prepared by:_____   Date:_____

Project Manager:_____   Date:_____

TITLE OF CHANGE:_____

DESCRIPTION OF CHANGE:

        Describe the change and resulting project
    modifications in order to accommodate the change.

PROJECT SCHEDULE IMPACT:

    Describe and quantify any anticipated change in the Project Schedule
    resulting from this change in Project Scope.

PROJECT COST IMPACT

    Describe and quantify any anticipated change in Project Cost
    resulting from this change in Project Scope.

Customer approval or disapproval to incorporate this change into the project is authorized by signature below and returning this document to the
office of the Project Manager. This Change Order is subject to all terms
and conditions of the original contract. This request becomes a Change
Order once approved, and work should commence immediately.

_____ Approved   _____
                           Customer Project Manager
_____ Disapproved   Date: _____

Form B-10 Use and Data Entry Guidelines

Purpose and Use

This form is used to maintain a project drawing list and also reflect the current status of each drawing on the list. This list must be continually maintained for each project. On the first working day of each month, each drawing list is updated (as necessary) and the new percent complete by drawing reflected.

Data Entry

Pertinent project information (self-explanatory) is entered at the top left corner of the form. The current issue date is placed opposite the next available report number in the upper center of the form. Directly beneath the upper right corner instructions, the total project percent design complete at the date of issue is entered.

Drawing numbers, title, and percent complete bars are entered below the project information. The percent complete bar is drawn from left to right in two sections: the first bar section indicates work done before last status report issue; and the second bar section indicates work done since the last status report issue. Percent complete guidelines for the bar chart are listed at the top of the form.

B-10

DRAWING LIST & STATUS REPORT

(COMPANY LOGO)

Project No._____

Customer_____

Sheet ____ of ____

Report No.	Issue Date	Report No.	Issue Date	PERCENT COMPLETE
1		7		■■■ Denotes work done as of last issue
2		8		⧄⧄⧄ Denotes work done since last issue
3		9		
4		10		30% Ready for Check
5		11		60% Checked & Backchecked
6		12		100% Issued for Construction

DRAWING NUMBER	DRAWING TITLE	Design % COMPLETE 0 10 20 30 40 50 60 70 80 90 100

Form B-11 Use and Data Entry Guidelines

Purpose and Use

This form is used to show the present status of project equipment. As such it is a historical report. The form is updated and issued on the first working day of each month the project is in progress.

Data Entry

Pertinent project information is entered at the top of the form (self-explanatory).

The equipment number, name with requisition/purchase order number (and revision) are listed in the left columns. The supplier and pertinent remarks are listed in the extreme right column.

The remainder of the columns are used to record dates that each activity (represented by the column headings) occurred.

B-11
EQUIPMENT STATUS REPORT

COMPANY LOGO

Project No. _____
Issue Date: _____
Page _____ of _____

PROJECT _____
LOCATION _____

EQUIP. NO.	DESCRIPTION	MR NO.	PO NO.- REV.	INQUIRY ISSUED Sch. / Act.	QUOTES REC'D. Sch. / Act.	BID TAB Sch. / Act.	RELEASE FOR P.O. Sch. / Act.	DELIVERY REQ'D. SITE	PROM. SHIP.	SHIPPED	SUPPLIER & REMARK

Form B-12 Use and Data Entry Guidelines

Purpose and Use

This form is used for formally requesting a project overrun for one or more control budget line items. No action can be taken by the purchasing department for a control budget line item that is expected to overrun until the overrun request is approved.

Data Entry

Pertinent project information and to/from data are entered at the top of the form (self-explanatory).

Each control budget line item expected to overrun which the project manager desires to purchase is listed with associated account code, control budget amount, quoted price (from selected vendor), and amount over budget (i.e., over the budget for that line item).

The steps taken to bring the expenditure within the budget prior to submittal of this form must be briefly described.

An overrun justification discussion or meeting must be held to determine a course of action. The result may be an overrun approval, or further investigation. If the overrun is approved, the project area absorbing the overrun will be noted with the general manager's signature at the bottom of the form. If further investigation is required, other alternatives to be evaluated and the target completion date for further evaluation will be noted with the general manager's signature at the bottom of the form.

INTERNAL MEMO

(COMPANY LOGO)

B-12

Date:_____

Page ___ of ___

PROJECT OVERRUN REQUEST

TO:_____   Customer:_____
General Manager

FROM:_____   Project No._____
Project Manager/Engineer

ADDITIONAL FUNDING (IN EXCESS OF LINE ITEM BUDGET VALUES) IS REQUESTED FOR THE FOLLOWING SERVICES/MATERIAL:

Account Code			Item Description	Control Budget Amount	Quoted Price	Amount Over Budget

DESCRIPTION OF STEPS TAKEN TO BRING THE EXPENDITURE WITHIN THE CONTROL BUDGET:

___ Overrun Approved

Overrun Absorbed By:

_____

_____

_____
General Manager

_____
Date

___ Evaluate the Following
Alternatives:

_____

_____

_____

_____

Written Alternative Evaluation
Report Submitted By:

_____

Form B-13 Use and Data Entry Guidelines

Purpose and Use

This form is used to record applied time of all personnel working on the project(s), which includes direct personnel, contract personnel, and consultant personnel. Applied time is spent by personnel working directly on any project. Personnel working on overhead functions (e.g., accounting, sales, marketing, and corporate management) do *not* fill out this form. The form is filled out daily, but submitted to the appropriate department managers on the first and sixteenth calendar days of each month. If either of these days falls on a weekend or holiday, the form is submitted on the following Monday or first working day following the holiday.

Data Entry

The employee name and number are filled in at the top of the form. For contract and consultant personnel, the employee number shall be the person's Social Security Number.

The period ending shall be either the fifteenth or the last day of the applicable month.

The first or sixteenth day of the month shall be placed under the word "Date" on the appropriate day for week No. 1 block. The subsequent days of the month up to the fifteenth or last day of the month shall be placed under the word "Date" under the associated weekday, using week No. 3 block if necessary. The month name shall be placed beside the word "Month" for each week block.

Six lines are allocated for each week block to record project numbers with associated hours worked. If a person has worked on more than one project or performed more than one work function (indicated by work code) multiple lines within each week block may be used. The work code is established by the chart of accounts.

Hours worked are totaled both at the bottom and right column on the form. Overtime hours (hourly personnel only) are also indicated in the right column.

Excused absence time is indicated at the bottom of the form and added to obtain total hours.

The form must be approved in the space provided at the bottom of the form.

B-13   **SEMI-MONTHLY TIME SHEET**

COMPANY LOGO

PERIOD ENDING ___ / ___ / ___

EMPLOYEE _____   EMPLOYEE NUMBER _____

PROJECT NO.	CHANGE ORDER NO.	WORK CODE	MON	TUE	WED	THU	FRI	SAT	SUN	TOTAL	OVER TIME

Month: (Date) — WEEK NO. 1

Month: (Date) — WEEK NO. 2

Month: (Date) — WEEK NO. 3

TOTAL HOURS WORKED

Excused Absence - Pay Requested

HOLIDAY										
VACATION										
SICK LEAVE										
MISC.										

TOTAL HOURS

Signature:_____   Approved By:_____

Date:_____   Date:_____

B-14

Page __ of __

MINUTES OF MEETING

COMPANY LOGO

Location:

Date:
Time:

Subject: PROJECT NAME
PROJECT NO.

MEETING SUBJECT

Attendees: COMPANY NAME   COMPANY NAME

Item	Description	Action
	PURPOSE OF MEETING STATEMENT	
	MEETING DISCUSSION BY ITEM, AND PERSONNEL ACTION WITH COMPLETION DATE	
	DECISIONS MADE IN MEETING	

B-15

PROJECT COST CONTROL PROGRAM

MONTHLY COST AND PROGRESS REPORT

MANAGEMENT SUMMARY

(PRIMARY ACCOUNTS)

(COMPANY LOGO)

Customer:
Project No:
Issue Date:

Account Code	Category or Item/Task Description	Initial Control Budget ($)	Customer Chg. Orders (Approved) ($)	Current Control Budget ($)	Committed Amount ($)	Budget Portion ($)	Cost Forecast ($)	Forecast Over+/ Under- ($)	Planned Comp. (%)	Actual Comp. (%)

B-16

PROJECT COST CONTROL PROGRAM
MONTHLY COST AND PROGRESS REPORT
MANAGEMENT SUMMARY
(SECONDARY ACCOUNTS)

COMPANY LOGO

Customer: _____

Project No: _____

Issue Date: _____

Account Code	Category or Item/Task Description	Initial Control Budget ($)	Customer Chg. Orders (Approved) ($)	Current Control Budget ($)	Committed Amount ($)	Budget Portion ($)	Cost Forecast ($)	Forecast Over+/ Under- ($)	Planned Comp. (%)	Actual Comp. (%)

B-17

PROJECT COST CONTROL PROGRAM
MONTHLY COST AND PROGRESS REPORT
PROJECT DATA
(TERTIARY ACCOUNTS)

COMPANY LOGO

Customer: _____
Project No: _____
Issue Date: _____

Account Code	Category or Item/Task Description	Initial Control Qty.	Initial Control Budget ($)	Customer Chg. Orders (Approved) ($)	Current Control Budget ($)	Commit. Qty.	Committed Capital ($)	Committed Freight ($)	Cost Forecast ($)	Forecast Over+/ Under- ($)	Planned Comp. (%)	Actual Comp. (%)

B-18

PROJECT COST CONTROL PROGRAM
MONTHLY COST AND PROGRESS REPORT
PREDICTED PROJECT OVERRUNS

Customer:
Project No:
Issue Date:

Account Code	Category or Item/Task Description	Initial Control Qty.	Initial Control Budget ($)	Customer Chg. Orders (Approved) ($)	Current Control Budget ($)	Commit. Qty.	Committed Capital ($)	Committed Freight ($)	Cost Forecast ($)	Forecast Over+/ Under- ($)	Planned Comp. (%)	Actual Comp. (%)

COMPANY LOGO

B-19

PROJECT COST CONTROL PROGRAM
MONTHLY COST AND PROGRESS REPORT
FIELD MATERIAL REPORT

COMPANY LOGO

Customer:

Project No:

Issue Date:

Account Code	Category or Item/Task Description	Vendor/ Supplier Name	Purchase Order or Contract Number	Promised Delivery Date	Predicted Delivery Date

B-20

PROJECT COST CONTROL PROGRAM
MONTHLY COST AND PROGRESS REPORT
VENDOR SUMMARY/EXPEDITING REPORT

COMPANY LOGO

Vendor Name	Purchase Order or Contract Number	Project Number	Account Code	Item Description	Committed Amount	Invoice Amount	Invoice Date	Promised Delivery Date	Predicted Delivery Date

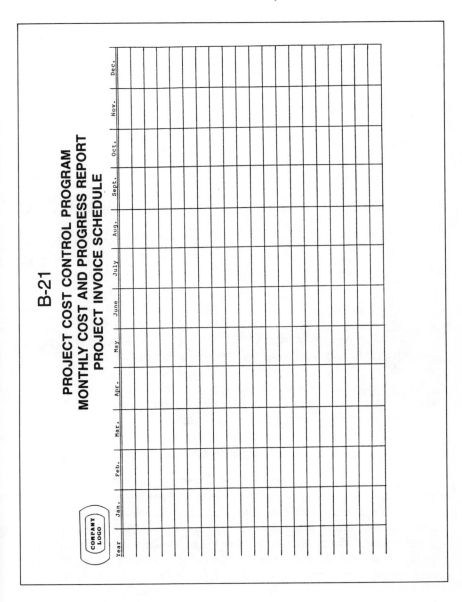

B-21

PROJECT COST CONTROL PROGRAM
MONTHLY COST AND PROGRESS REPORT
PROJECT INVOICE SCHEDULE

Appendix C
Example Application
of the RIICH Technique

To assist in the application of the RIICH technique for developing a program cost control program, as described in Chapter 2, the following example has been developed. The example utilizes and closely references information presented in Chapters 2 and 4; therefore, it is necessary that the reader have thoroughly reviewed these chapters. The five-step procedure outlined in Chapter 2 is followed.

Example Problem

Management of a small (e.g., 30 to 50 persons) engineering and constuction company, ABC Corporation, has recently recognized that inaccuracy in corporate profit planning has become unacceptable. Project cost forecasts and/or overruns are causing corporate profit forecasters to make dramatic changes on a monthly basis. Management presently uses project cost control procedures accumulated from employee preservice experience. Management's first attempt at solving the problem was to place a computer software firm under contract utilizing a "systems analyst" to examine the problem. This approach has proven to be expensive and has yielded only marginal improvement. Management next decided to hire a permanent cost control engineer to improve the system. After a six-month period this approach also was not fruitful. Since the company is young (e.g., in business less than six years), management has not had the opportunity (due to rapid growth) to be involved in either of the two attempted solutions after each was initiated. Instead, management coincidentally adopted a "stop-gap" measure of requiring that all purchasing authority be placed at the corporate management level. This was done with the idea that those in corporate management are the original personnel who started the company and effectively controlled costs in the early years. However, even this step is not a permanent solution if the company expects to continue to grow.

At this point ABC Corporation's management is at a loss as to how to solve the problem and is wondering if every engineering and construction company is faced with the same dilemma. Consequently, management is wondering if it is possible to do any better, or are dramatic forecast profit fluctuations part of the nature of the business?

The RIICH Solution

To assist ABC Corporation, management must first accept several basic premises:

☐ A project cost control program is a management system.
☐ Project cost control is only successful if corporate management is continuously involved.
☐ Project cost control procedure problems are solved by a management system analyst (i.e., someone who has management experience and insight).
☐ Placing purchasing authority at the top management level is only a partial solution at best. Normally, internal manpower cost overruns are as significant a problem as overruns on purchased items.

Using a converging project cost control program developed through application of the RIICH technique, ABC Corporation will be capable of reliably forecasting corporate profit (as is affected by project costs) within acceptable limits (i.e., ±10%). ABC Corporation applies the RIICH technique as follows:

Step 1—Review

An ABC Corporation organizational chart is illustrated in Figure C-1. As is normal, the informal functional organization may be somewhat different; however, the formal organization at the upper management level, as presented, is what is needed to apply the RIICH technique.

ABC Corporation has existing, written cost and schedule control procedures that must be reviewed in depth before any employees are interviewed. It is important for the interviewer to know what was intended by the written procedures before he is told what procedures are actually in use. Through use of the written procedures and employee interviews, work flow paths illustrated in Figures C-2 through C-6 are developed. Those flow path elements shown as dotted are the elements missing from the flow paths that were recommended in Chapter 4.

The work flow path charts are organized in the two basic areas of ABC Corporation project responsibility—sales and project management. The organizational chart and work flow path charts (Figures C-1 through C-6) are now distributed to ABC Corporation management. A meeting is held with corporate management to confirm the flow path charts and firmly establish with management this specific baseline to which recommended changes can be made. *It is essential to establish this baseline.* The result of application of the RIICH technique is typically only a 10 to 20% modification of existing corporate work flow paths. Without establishing such a baseline it is very difficult to show that 80 to 90% of the original path elements are incorporated in the resulting system. The realization

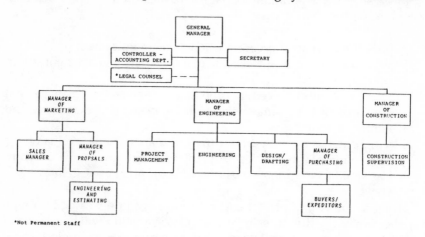

Figure C-1. ABC Corporation organizational chart.

by corporate management and employees that the majority of the existing work flow paths remain unchanged is very important to system acceptance.

Step 2—Integration

The fundamentals presented in Chapter 4 are now integrated into the organizational chart and work flow paths established in Step 1. It is very important that the checks and balances discussed in Chapter 4 be adopted. However, it must be noted that these checks and balances may be achieved in more than one manner. Organization and work flow paths discussed in Chapter 4, Figures 4-1 through 4-6 are only one method of achieving these checks and balances. The impact of integra-

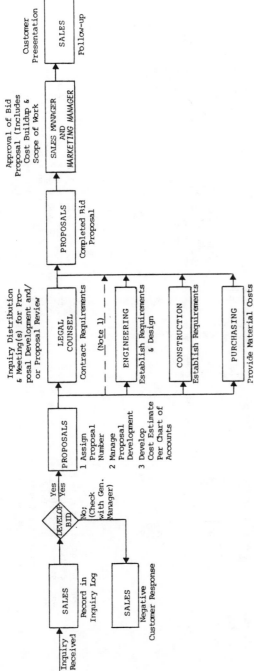

Figure C-2.   Sales work flow path—Proposal phase.

NOTES: (1)   If an inquiry is very similar to a past project, the estimate is sometimes factored from previous historical project cost data and the proposal developed without the assistance of other departments.

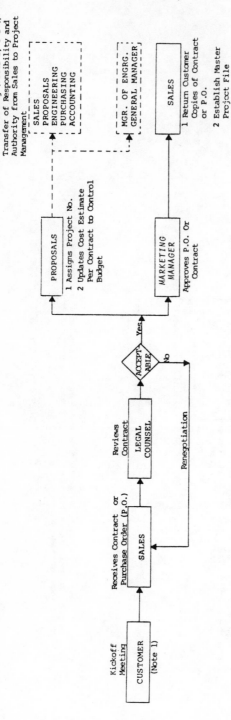

NOTES:

(1) Does not occur for each project.

(2) Project Management (PM) Instructions includes a written Transmittal, Control Budget, Proposal, Contract or P.O. and Customer Specifications, as a minimum. Upon acceptance (within two weeks) of the PM Instructions by the Manager of Engineering, the PM Instructions Transmittal is signed and returned to Sales.

(3) This may not be a formal meeting; all material may be handed directly to the Manager of Engineering.

(4) A copy of the PM Instructions is retained by Proposals in order to provide a budget check, per Figure 3-5.

Figure C-3. Sales work flow path—After sale phase.

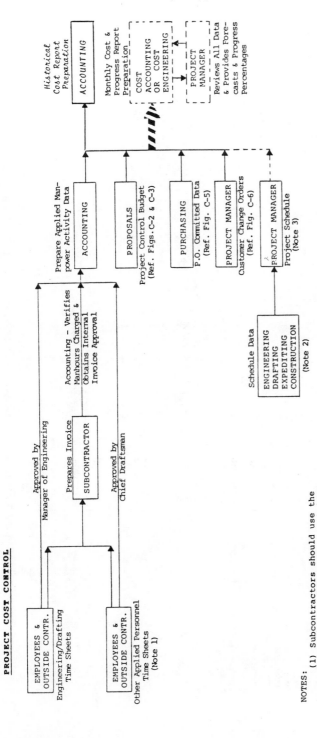

Figure C-4. Project management work flow path—Project cost control.

PROJECT COST CONTROL

EMPLOYEES &
OUTSIDE CONTR.
Engineering/Drafting
Time Sheets

EMPLOYEES &
OUTSIDE CONTR.
Other Applied Personnel
Time Sheets
(Note 1)

Approved by
Manager of Engineering

Prepares Invoice

SUBCONTRACTOR

Approved by
Chief Draftsman

Accounting – Verifies
Manhours Charged &
Obtains Internal
Invoice Approval

Schedule Data

ENGINEERING
DRAFTING
EXPEDITING
CONSTRUCTION

(Note 2)

Historical
Cost Report
Preparation

ACCOUNTING

Monthly Cost &
Progress Report
Preparation

COST
ACCOUNTING
OR COST
ENGINEERING

PROJECT
MANAGER

Reviews All Data
& Provides Fore-
casts & Progress
Percentages

Prepare Applied Man-
power Activity Data

ACCOUNTING

PROPOSALS

Project Control Budget
(Ref. Figs. C-2 & C-3)

PURCHASING

P.O. Committed Data
(Ref. Fig. C-5)

PROJECT MANAGER

Customer Change Orders
(Ref. Fig. C-6)

PROJECT MANAGER

Project Schedule
(Note 3)

NOTES:

(1) Subcontractors should use the
     same time sheet for invoicing.

(2) Data provided primarily by the
     Equipment Status Report, Drawing
     List & Status Report and Construction
     Reports.

(3) Project Manager may use a simple bar chart
     or one of the computer CPM techniques.

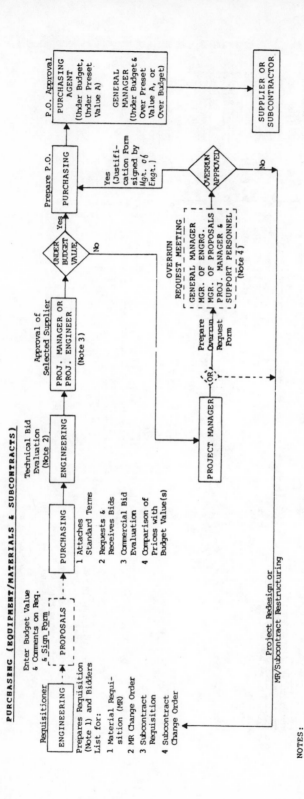

Figure C-5. Project management work flow path—Purchasing (equipment/materials and subcontracts).

NOTES:

(1) Includes Detail Material List or Scope of Work.

(2) No more than three bids should be provided for technical evaluation unless more are requested.

(3) Written approval on the designated form.

(4) May be taken care of in the Monthly Project Meetings (includes discussion of alternatives and impact on the project).

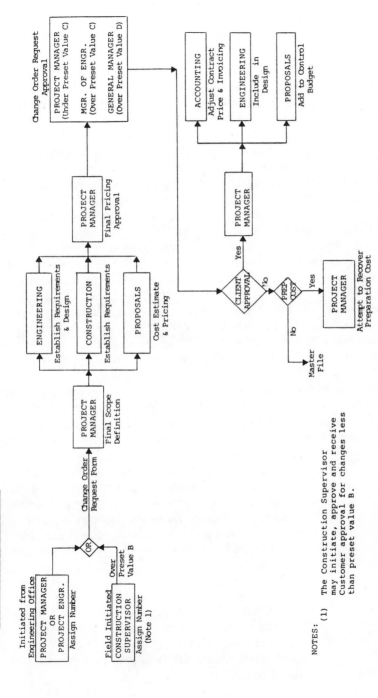

Figure C-6. Project management work flow path—Customer change orders.

tion on each figure will be discussed separately. Those work flow elements not present in ABC Corporation but required to establish a minimum necessary for project cost control success are indicated with *.

Figure C-1—Existing Organizational Chart. Making a comparison between Figure C-1 and Figure 4-1 indicates the following differences that have an impact on the ability to control project cost:

☐ The sales manager and manager of proposals both report to an intermediate level manager of marketing. Since the primary responsibility of the manager of marketing is sales volume with a secondary emphasis on profit margin, this arrangement eliminates one check and balance element that could be present. If the sales manager and manager of proposals both report to the general manager, there may be a more equal emphasis on sales volume/profit margin and product quality, thereby reducing pressure to decrease cost to enhance sales volume. This situation sometimes causes project estimates to become unrealistic, thereby eventually resulting in project overruns. This balance between sacrifice of quality and sales volume as it relates to market competitiveness can only equitably be established by the person responsible for the total picture—the general manager. However, other organizational schemes to achieve the same result are possible.

☐ *The manager of purchasing reports to the manager of engineering. Again, a significant check and balance element may be lost. The manager of engineering's primary interest is "getting a quality job done." In many instances, he may consider item cost overruns to be justifiable sacrifices when it appears that purchase of a less expensive item would cause schedule slippage. This may occur even when the primary interest of the manager of purchasing is to purchase a quality item within the budget allocated. With the manager of purchasing reporting to the general manager, a more equitable evaluation of the tradeoff between cost overrun and schedule slippage is possible. The manager of engineering and manager of purchasing can then each retain their primary concerns.

Each of these two differences from the organizational structure shown in Figure 4-1 individually do not constitute a major flaw in ABC Corporation's ability to control costs. However, these organizational weaknesses, coupled with the following work flow path weaknesses, may result in a loss of project cost control.

Figure C-2—Sales Work Flow Path (Proposal Phase).

☐ *In reviewing this work flow path, it was found to be very similar to that recommended in Figure 4-2. The one difference is that the marketing manager in conjunction with the sales manager approves the proposal before it is presented to the customer. This approval should always include the person ultimately responsible for total project performance—the general manager. Consequently, only this one modification to this work flow path will be necessary.

Figure C-3—Sales Work Flow Path (After Sale Phase). A comparison of Figure C-3 and Figure 4-3 indicates the following differences that may affect project cost control:

☐ The manager of marketing approves the customer's purchase order. The person ultimately responsible for the project, the general manager, should constitute the final purchase order approval. Again, the emphasis at this time should be on performance, not sales volume. Acceptance of contract term modifications can easily affect project costs. However, approval by the manager of engineering may jeopardize the sale in terms of time.

☐ *No formal documentation or procedure exists to transfer project responsibility from the sales function to the project management function. Since "time is money," especially on project work, it is very important for sales to offer a clear, concise project description and budget to project management. It is equally important that project management accept the responsibility. Normally, a formal PM meeting, as discussed in Chapter 4, is the easiest method for transfer of responsibility.

Figure C-4—Project Management Work Flow Path (Project Cost Control). ABC Corporation presently has a program intended to control project costs. The work flow path for this program is illustrated in Figure C-4. A comparison of Figures C-4 and 4-4 indicates the following differences that may affect project cost control:

☐ *Reporting of all cost data to the accounting department, which subsequently publishes an "after-the-fact" historical cost report. This work flow element tends to eliminate two vital work flow characteristics—interaction between the project manager and the cost reporting function, and cost counseling between those who collect the data and management. The project manager should provide data for, approve and be ultimately responsible for timely publication of any cost and/or progress report describing his project. He should also counsel with those preparing the report on the accuracy of each line item value, especially forecasts. The existing ABC Corporation cost engineer should be assigned the task of data collection and preparation of the monthly cost and progress report and advise management if all elements of the adopted project cost control program are continually and properly followed.

☐ *Disassociation of project schedule data from project cost data. Typically, project managers are very closely associated with schedule data, since it is collected and schedules prepared all within the engineering group. However, this is not true concerning cost data. Therefore, the input of schedule data into project cost reporting is very important, since cost and schedule are interdependent.

Figure C-5—Project Management Work Flow Path (Purchasing). A comparison of Figures C-5 and 4-5 indicates the following differences that may affect project cost control:

☐ *Direct submittal of requisitions to purchasing. It is very important to the success of any project cost control program that all requisitions for purchase be compared with the current control budget by the preparer of that budget—the proposal group. For many budget line items, the original intention at project inception was never written down. This check and balance element tends to continually reintegrate original project thinking into the project in progress.

☐ *Review of line item cost overruns by the project manager. If a budget line item cost is intended to be overrun, this should be openly recognized prior to the occurence not only by the project manager, but, as a minimum, also by his immediate superior. This may easily be accomplished by use of an overrun request form and overrun request meeting, as indicated in Figure 4-5.

☐ The manager of engineering approves overrun requests. It is important that the person responsible for the overall project performance (the general manager) approve each overrun request. Approval by upper management will have the effect of causing the employee to exhaust all avenues before requesting a line item overrun.

Figure C-6—Project Management Work Flow Path (Customer Change Order). In reviewing this work flow path, it was found to be very similar to that recommended in Figure 4-6. Consequently very few, if any, modifications to this work flow path should be necessary.

These proposed work flow path modifications (approximately 20% adjustments) should be clearly indicated on the charts developed in Step 1 and again formally distributed to corporate management. A meeting with management should be held to discuss and adopt the recommended changes. It should be noted here that the proposed work flow path modifications may be again changed by agreement within ABC Corporation management, but the new work flow must accomplish the intended check and balances or the project cost control program will not improve.

Once the work flow paths are agreed to by ABC Corporation management, the paths should be reduced to a set of written procedures. These procedures should include reference to and examples of the forms necessary to accomplish the intent of the project cost control program. Examples of such forms are available in Appendix B.

Step 3—Implementation

Implementation of the project cost control program modifications consists of assistance in familiarizing all personnel through counseling and training and assistance in application. As with any policy change, initial employee resistance will be considered high to those working closely with the program modifications. However, as each employee understands that the converging nature of the program eventually makes their job easier, program acceptance becomes easy and work efficiency improves.

A second feature of implementation is reconciling the cost data reporting technique with an accounting general ledger system. Since ABC Corporation is a young, privately-owned company, the accounting system was able to adapt to the general chart of accounts format and detail.

Step 4—Computerization

ABC Corporation is, at present, primarily involved in project management and design, which includes construction management through subcontracting. This business activity in conjunction with a smaller number of personnel does not indicate the need for computerization to facilitate data handling. Management feels that manual data manipulation will be efficient. However, if the company expands to include more personnel, or begins to order and coordinate construction commodity materials, computerization will become necessary. This decision follows the guideline shown in Figure 2-2.

Step 5—Habit

Now that the project cost control program has been implemented, the control of project costs will become an unconscious habit. Like the convergence of the curves presented in Figure 2-3, project costs for each newly completed project will more closely coincide with the project budget, thereby providing ease of profit forecasting and accuracy in new project estimating (through the use of accurate historical costs). With availability of historical data from the completion of each successive project using this project cost control program, corporate project forecasting and costs will more closely converge to project budgets.

Summary

This example centers around cost control problems encountered by a smaller engineering and construction company. The example has shown how application of the RIICH technique makes it possible to regain control of project costs. However, the RIICH technique can also be used to improve cost control for larger engineering and construction companies and for operating and manufacturing companies.

One such scenario is an older, established (e.g., 20 to 50 years in business) company using a computerized project cost control program, which has in recent years encountered unacceptable profit forecasting variations that can be attributed to inaccurate project cost forecasts. In this case, each step would be much more involved, since the company would probably be considerably larger (e.g., more than 100 people). However, the RIICH technique would provide a sound method of improving project cost control.

Index

H

Habit, 12
  application of the RIICH technique, 152
Heat transfer equipment, example chart of accounts, 94
Historical cost data/report, 10, 12, 19, 22, 67, 84, 149

I

Implementation, 12
  application of the RIICH technique, 151
Indirect costs, 19
  example chart of accounts, 89
Initial control budget, 19, 24, 34, 67–68
Initial control quantity, 19
Inspection and testing, example chart of accounts, 87, 89, 98
Installation
  building, structural steel, piping, instrumentation and controls, electrical, example chart of accounts, 89, 101–4
Instrumentation
  example chart of accounts, 89, 96, 97
  numbering system, 46
Insulation, example chart of accounts, 90, 105
Insurance, example chart of accounts, 90, 106
Integration, 11
  application of the RIICH technique, 142
Investment security, 2
Invoice
  detail or predicted on reports, 75, 139
  numbering system, 42
  schedule, 83
  vendor/subcontractor, 39

K

"Keep it simple," 48, 53
Kickoff meeting, 32

L

Labor burden costs, 19
Language barrier, 16
Lead/lag time, 60
Letter numbering system, 48
Line item, 19, 21, 150
Loading. See Packaging/crating, loading, and transportation.
Lubricants, fuels, and chemicals, example chart of accounts, 97

M

Major equipment, example chart of accounts, 88, 94–95
"Make-up syndrome," 66, 83
Manager of engineering, 37. See also Project cost control responsibility.
Management. See also Work flow path/procedure, project management.
  communication with sales, 24
  reports, 74, 81ff.
  role in cost control program, 1, 8ff., 141
  role in planning/scheduling, 55, 66–67
Management summary, 78–79, 81
Manpower
  cost estimating, 68
  data handling, 76
Manual data manipulation, 10, 12, 76–77
Master file, project, 33

N

O

P

Notes